Knitting in Tuscany

Nicky Epstein

Knitting in Tuscany

fabulous design
luscious yarns
shopping secrets
food & wine
travel notes

Nicky
Epstein
Books
An imprint of Sixth&Spring Books

This book is dedicated to my wonderful Italian grandparents, Annuccia and Aniello DeFazio.

Note: We have made every effort to ensure the accuracy of the information in this book, but addresses and other information are subject to change, so doublecheck with hotels, restaurants, museums and other businesses before you travel.

Managing Editor: Wendy Williams
Senior Editor: Michelle Bredeson
Art Director: Diane Lamphron
Associate Art Director: Sheena T. Paul
Yarn Editor: Tanis Gray
Instructions Editor: Eve Ng
Instructions Proofreaders: Jordana Jacobs, Nancy Henderson
Technical Illustrations: Peggy Greig, Jane Fay
Copy Editor: Kristina Sigler

Vice President, Publisher: Trisha Malcolm
Creative Director: Joe Vior
Production Manager: David Joinnides
President: Art Joinnides

Fashion Photography:
Rose Callahan
Still Life Photography:
Jack Deutsch Studio, David Lazarus
Fashion Stylist: Julie Hines
Hair and Makeup: Ingeborg K.
Personal Travel Photography:
Howard and Nicky Epstein

Library of Congress Control Number: 2008936333
ISBN: 978-1-933027-75-3
Manufactured in China
1 3 5 7 9 10 8 6 4 2
First Edition

Nicky
Epstein
Books

An imprint of Sixth&Spring Books
233 Spring Street, New York, NY 10013
www.sixthandspringbooks.com

CONTENTS

INTRODUCTION 6
WHY TUSCANY? 8
KNITTING IN TUSCANY: A SHORT HISTORY 10

Beautiful cities, fabulous designs

FLORENCE 14
❖ Dante's Beatrice Shawl 22
❖ Wool Guild Wreath 24
❖ Medici Scarf 30
❖ Pinocchio 32

SIENA, MONTERIGGIONI AND SAN GIMIGNANO 36
❖ Siena Rooftop Sweater 44
❖ Della Robbia Flower Pillows 48
❖ Fresco Vest 52
❖ Cypress Capelet 60
❖ Carrara Marble Cardigan 64

CHIANTI 68
❖ Chianti Rooster Pillow 74
❖ Cashmere Necklette 78
❖ Vineyard Bag 80

MONTEPULCIANO, MONTALCINO AND CORTONA 82
❖ Abbondanza Wrap 90
❖ Bella Bride's Dress 92
❖ Felted Etruscan Pitcher 98
❖ Tuscan Sun Shawl 102

TUSCAN FOOD AND WINE 104
KNITTER-FRIENDLY RECIPES 107
NICKY'S TRAVEL TIPS 108
❖ Yarn and Notions Resources 109
❖ Abbreviations, Skill Levels, Photo Credits 110
❖ Knitting and Embroidery Techniques 111
❖ Acknowledgments 112

INTRODUCTION

Michelangelo, Leonardo, Dante, Boccaccio, de' Medici, Donatello, Epstein...Epstein??

What's an Epstein doing among these giants of Tuscany? I'm eating, I'm drinking, I'm *knitting!* This book is a knitter's guide to Tuscany, for those who actually go there or just want to enjoy it vicariously. Needless to say, it was a great pleasure writing this book, in which I get to share the joys of the region and point out special features of interest for knitters.

I'll take you to unique knitting shops, we'll visit a legendary knitting mill, take an insider's look at the Pitti Filati (Florence's famous knitting trade show) and even travel to a cashmere farm run by an expatriate American. We'll explore the great cities—Florence and Siena—with their grand piazzas, world-class art museums and monuments. We'll ramble through fantastic little hill towns like Montepulciano, Cortona and the villages of the Chianti region, each with its own charming personality, festivals and some of the world's best wines. I'll give you a brief history of knitting in Tuscany and share with you some of the facts I've learned about Italian yarn and the magic it holds for so many knitters around the world.

In addition, I'll give you some personal recommendations for hotels, restaurants, places of interest and great shopping finds, as well as an overview of traditional Tuscan foods and wines. I even share a few of my favorite Italian-style recipes and some tips to help make your trip as smooth and enjoyable as possible. And, finally, I've designed fifteen knit pieces (with patterns) inspired by my travels in Tuscany that I hope you'll enjoy knitting, whether you're sitting over a cappuccino in the Piazza della Signoria in Florence or having an iced tea on your front porch in Des Moines.

Welcome to glorious, magical Tuscany. *Mangiate, bevete, lavorate a maglia!* (Eat, drink, knit!)

Grazie,
Nicoletta DeFazio Quinones Epstein

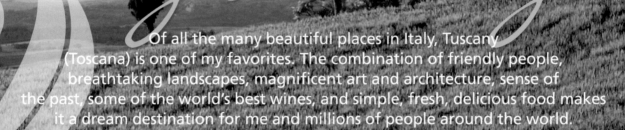

Why Tuscany?

Of all the many beautiful places in Italy, Tuscany (Toscana) is one of my favorites. The combination of friendly people, breathtaking landscapes, magnificent art and architecture, sense of the past, some of the world's best wines, and simple, fresh, delicious food makes it a dream destination for me and millions of people around the world.

Tuscany lies in central Italy and boasts seascapes, rolling hills, snowcapped mountains and exquisite views punctuated by dramatic cypress trees. The region covers 8,880 square miles (22,990 square km) and is divided into ten provinces. A sense of history dominates the area; the Renaissance feels far from remote. The treasure-filled cities and quaint and charming hill towns offer an unending variety of wonderful surprises for all the senses.

Tuscans are proud of a heritage that goes back to the enigmatic Etruscans (an ancient society of artistically and scientifically advanced people that predates the Romans), and many faces you see in Tuscany today could have come straight out of an Etruscan fresco. Tuscans celebrate their past with festivals, pageantry and civic pride. The center of activity in a Tuscan town is the piazza, and it is the hub for the *passeggiata* (evening stroll), when Tuscans discuss the day's activities, visit with neighbors and perhaps have a glass of *vino*.

Tuscany's architecture runs the gamut from Romanesque to Gothic to Renaissance to Baroque, and all of these styles blend beautifully to create a distinctively Tuscan look.

Tuscany has a rich heritage of art. Many patrons of the arts have encouraged artists over the centuries, and the list of luminaries is stunning: Pisano, Brunelleschi, Ghiberti, Donatello, della Robbia, Leonardo, Raphael, Michelangelo and Cellini are just a few of the celebrated artists who lived and worked in Tuscany. Renaissance frescoes (paintings executed on damp, freshly laid plaster) are seen throughout Tuscany on the walls of public buildings, churches, palaces and tombs.

But with all of Tuscany's rich heritage of art and literature, perhaps the most memorable experience is simply driving through the amazing countryside with the Tuscan sun painting the landscape of hills, mountains and valleys into dreamscapes that will never leave your memory.

Life is but a dream...
A typically beautiful Tuscan farm with
the ever-present cypress trees.

Knitting in Tuscany

A SHORT HISTORY

Tuscany has a rich tradition of knitting, wool and textiles that goes back centuries, and that tradition has endured to make Italy one of the main fashion centers of the world. Today's luxurious men's suits, designer knitwear for women, and a rainbow of glorious knitting yarns are the results of Tuscany's long love affair with wool.

No one knows for sure, but many experts agree that knitting began in the Middle East about 850 years ago, probably in Egypt, where remnants of decorative socks have been found (Nefertiti Knits?). It is believed that the craft was transported by traders and merchants from Egypt to Spain to France and then to Italy, where folks really ran with it. Some of the early evidence of knitting in Italy can be found in a number of knitting Madonna paintings from around 1350. In a famous painting by Lorenzetti, the Madonna is knitting in the round with four needles.

One huge influence on the history of Tuscany was the success of wool traders and merchants who imported raw wool (especially merino) from England and Spain, as well as the success of the textile workers who cleaned, carded (brushed raw or washed fibers), spun, dyed and wove the wool into high-quality cloth. The center of this activity was Florence. Over the years, the wool merchants became immensely wealthy and formed the Wool Guild (Arte della Lana), which wielded enormous sway over all aspects of Tuscan life. The Wool Guild supervised all the activities of textile production from raw wool to finished cloth, at one time employing one third of Florence's population in the wool trades. The artist Andrea della Robbia (his father was a member of the guild) created the Wool

The early days

Clockwise from top: *Summer* by Italian painter Francesco Bassano depicts the sheep-shearing season; the engraving *Villanella* by Charles François Jalabert shows an Italian girl knitting; artist Andrea della Robbia's coat of arms for the Wool Guild.

EXPLORING
A Museum for Knitters

Prato, a city located northwest of Florence, owes its growth and wealth to the textile industry. To celebrate this heritage, the city built the Museo del Tessuto (Textile Museum; Via Santa Chiara 24; museodeltessuto.it), which will be of great interest to all knitters. It has over 6,000 samples of fabric from all over the globe, spanning ancient to modern times, as well as costumes and a great collection of textile-weaving machines.

Guild's striking glazed terra-cotta emblem in 1487, which can still be seen in the Museo dell'Opera del Duomo in Florence. (I've created a knitted version of the emblem in this book to honor those wool-driven artistic visionaries; see page 24.) The father of the celebrated sculptor Donatello was a wool carder, and did you know that Columbus (who wasn't from Tuscany, but let's not split fibers) was the son of a wool weaver? (Chris would have probably become one too, if he hadn't been bitten by the travel bug.)

With its idealistic yearnings and generous patronage, the Wool Guild was a driving force behind the formation of the Renaissance. The Renaissance, which means "rebirth" (*Rinascimento* in Italian), was a period of great artistic and intellectual progress. It began in Tuscany at the end of the 14th century and was centered in Florence and Siena. During this golden age, some of the greatest artists and thinkers of history, including Botticelli, Leonardo, Michelangelo and Machiavelli, flourished. The Medici of Florence were one of the most influential families in the Wool Guild and the most powerful and influential patrons of artists, architects and scientists in the Renaissance.

Although most of Tuscany's wool now comes from Australia, New Zealand and a rapidly growing Chinese wool market, its successful, innovative mills and designers keep the region at the center of the fiber, textile and knitting world. So as you enjoy the glories of Tuscany, don't forget the contribution of the humble sheep to its beautiful evolution. Not baaaaad!●

A Visit to the Pitti Filati

Twice a year, the Pitti Immagine Filati (aka Pitti Filati) is held in Florence at the impressive Fortezza da Basso. It is the premier international event and trade show for the knitting industry. There are more than 150 exhibitors, and thousands of designers and buyers from fashion houses, yarn companies, knitwear magazines, yarn mills and knitwear collection manufacturers attend. The show is open only to the trade, but I've been lucky enough to attend twice, once as a buying consultant for an international yarn company and once to do research for this book, and I'll give you an insider's glimpse.

The show is the harbinger of what is to come in terms of colors, textures, stitches and styling for knitters. One of the highlights of the show is the color preview room. When I was last there for the 2008/2009 show, this room held a dazzling array of knitted cakes, pies, pastries and candy that looked good enough to eat. The autumn/winter color lines had titles like "Pastry," "Dark Chocolate" and "Candy," and everyone received a beautiful color card with the actual colored yarns.

Throughout the show are wonderful exhibits of knitted garments and items that range from high fashion to high camp (I even saw a knitted commode), and you can walk around the exhibit all day long without ever getting bored. There are displays, seminars and workshops, but most importantly, business is conducted.

Behind semi-closed doors, negotiations for the purchase of yarns and fabric take place. Yarn companies (which sell to yarn shops) from around the world negotiate with yarn manufacturers and mills in an effort to obtain a proprietary line of yarns, and knit fashions are purchased, in the form of swatches, by magazines, designers and manufacturers.

The most frenetic activity happens at the swatch booths. The yarn manufacturers and yarn mills exhibit eye-catching knitted garments from some of the most talented international designers in order to sell yarn and set the trends for the forthcoming season. The swatches are actually beautiful designer garments knit in child-size proportions. Hundreds of buyers, magazine editors and others swarm the booths trying to purchase the garments that will be in fashion next season. The manufacturers who run the booths are highly protective of their designs, and photographs are discouraged, but there were many areas in which photography was allowed. There is a competition amongst the buyers, but it is a cordial one.

This show always sets my creative juices bubbling. To find out more about it, visit pittimmagine.com.●

❖ Pitti Party

The world of knitting convenes twice a year at the Pitti Filati to determine what knitters everywhere will be knitting next year. The many exhibitions range from outstanding to outrageous.

Florence's Ponte Vecchio on the river Arno is one of the city's most iconic sights.

Florence

If I were to attempt to write about all the art, architecture, sightseeing, hotels, restaurants, shopping, people and myriad other joys of visiting **FLORENCE**, it would fill entire books more ambitious than this one. Instead, I will share with you just a few of my personal favorites and trust you'll fill in your itinerary with further research.

Florence (Firenze), the capital of Tuscany, is the birthplace of the Renaissance and possesses perhaps the greatest wealth of Western art and architecture in the world. It is a wonderful city to walk around in; with a good map, it's easy to find the sights, shops and restaurants described here. And if you do get lost, you might not want to be found.

ACCOMODATIONS

Hotel Loggiato dei Serviti (Piazza SS. Annunziata 3; loggiatodeiservitihotel.it) is housed in a sixteenth-century former convent on a lovely square. It boasts nice furnishings and amenities and vaulted ceilings. **Hotel Torre Guelfa** (Borgo SS. Apostoli 8; hoteltorreguelfa.com) is located in a fourteenth-century towered building near the Ponte Vecchio. It features beautiful views, canopied beds and a pleasant Florentine ambiance. **Grand Hotel Baglioni** (Piazza Unità Italiana 6; hotelbaglioni.it) is a large but charming hotel I stayed at when I attended the Pitti Filati. The rooms are good-sized and have traditional Florentine furnishings; some have great views of the Duomo. There is a restaurant on the top floor with windows overlooking the city. Even if you don't stay here, I highly recommend visiting the roof for a drink and enjoying one of the best 360-degree panoramas in all of Florence.

DINING

So many restaurants, so little time. My favorite, **La Giostra** (Borgo Pinti 12r; ristorantelagiostra.com), has great Tuscan/Austrian food, an extensive wine list and is fun, fun, fun. Most of the fun is supplied by owner Dimitri Kunz d'Asburgo Lorena, a Hapsburg prince, who runs this special place along with his two sons and a daughter. Dimitri traverses the restaurant in his chef's hat serving bread, pouring wine and schmoozing with patrons in many languages. The menu has wonderful dishes, like a colorful appetizer of *crostini misti,* osso buco, tagliatelle with truffles, and an enormous and delicious Wiener schnitzel. La Giostra is probably the only restaurant in Tuscany where you have a choice of tiramisu or Sacher torte for dessert. At **Le Fonticine** (Via Nazionale 79r; lefonticine.com), a country-style trattoria, opt for the rear dining room, which is lined with the owner's colorful paintings. This is a great place to try Florentine beefsteak, along with items like *insalata caprese,* fried zucchini blossoms and pasta with mushrooms and truffle sauce. **Osteria del Cinghiale Bianco** (Borgo San Jacopo 43r; cinghialebianco.it) is a delightful casual dining spot located in a fourteenth-century building. Be prepared to dine on hearty *cinghiale* (wild boar) with polenta and classic Tuscan dishes of veal, chicken and pasta. Order a red or white house wine—it's poured from ceramic boar's-head pitchers. **Trattoria ZàZà** (Piazza del Mercato Centrale 26r; trattoriazaza.it) is a lively little trattoria located right across from the Mercato Centrale (Central Market). It is filled with market workers and tourists alike enjoying dishes like *ribollita,* ravioli with spinach and truffles and stewed beans. I like to sit outdoors and enjoy some people-watching under a tented area where waitresses scurry by with mouthwatering dishes. The restaurant list goes on and on, and don't forget the gelato shops. Many say **Vivoli** (Via Isole delle Stinche 7r) is the best, but I prefer **Il Granduca** (Via del Calzaiuoli 59). You'll have fun deciding on your own favorites.

There are not enough hours in a day (or a lifetime) to experience all the joys of this beautiful city, from great art to great food to great shopping.

This is a short and very personal selection out of a neverending list of outstanding places to visit in beautiful Florence. Information on all of the museums mentioned here can be found on one Web site: polomuseale.firenze.it. The **Galleria dell'Accademia** (Via Ricasoli 58–60) houses Michelangelo's *David,* the world's most famous sculpture. It may seem like the longest line in the world to get in, but you know you've got to see it. When I first visited the *David* years ago, as an aspiring artist, I had an epiphany viewing this perfect work of art carved from a damaged block of marble. In the Galleria you'll also find other great works by Perugino, Giambologna and Botticelli. The **Galleria degli Uffizi** (Piazzale degli Uffizi) is one of the greatest art museums in the world and is crammed with masterpieces by Michelangelo, Leonardo, Botticelli, Titian, Raphael, Caravaggio (one of my favorites, with his chiaroscuro style depicting dramatic contrast between light and shadow) and many others. You won't find a painting of dogs playing poker at this venue. **Museo Nazionale del Bargello** (Via del Proconsolo 4), also known as the Palazzo del Popolo (Palace of the People), is a Gothic building that once served as a barracks and prison, and the building itself is almost as interesting as the masterpieces it contains. You'll find Michelangelo's *Bacchus,* terra-cottas by Giovanni della Robbia (I created pillows inspired by his work on page 48) and a whole room of Donatello sculptures, among many other great works of art. **Palazzo Pitti** (Piazza dei Pitti) is located in the Oltrarno quarter of Florence, across the Arno river from the historical area of Florence. This beautifully frescoed Medici palace is home to thousands of paintings from the likes of Raphael, Rubens, Titian and many others. Be sure to visit the Medici apartments, the costume gallery (of particular interest to knitters), the decorative arts collection and the lavish Boboli Gardens in back of the palace. **Santa Maria del Fiore** (Piazza del

Stitch among the treasures
The classic statues offer pointers as I knit at the Museo Nazionale del Bargello.

Duomo; www.operaduomo.firenze.it), Florence's cathedral, which is known as the **Duomo,** towers above the city's skyline. The enormous structure, with its cladding of white, green and pink marble and crowned by Brunelleschi's magnificent dome, is amazing and belies its spare interior. Nearby is the beautiful **Campanile,** a bell tower designed by Giotto, rising 277.9 feet feet above the ground, with 414 steps to the top. (Although I hear the view from the top is awesome, I opted for the view from the roof of the Hotel Baglioni, where I enjoyed my knitting while having a glass of wine.) The highlight of the Duomo's **Baptistry of St. John** is Lorenzo Ghiberti's East Doors, with ten gilded bronze depictions of Old Testament scenes. At age 22, Ghiberti won the commission for the doors after a competition against some of the finest Florentine artists of the day. The competition was sponsored by the prestigious Wool Guild (let's hear it for the Wool Guild!). When Michelangelo saw the doors he said, "They are so beautiful that they would grace the entrance to Paradise," giving them the nickname "the Gates of Paradise." The **Ponte**

Florence Yarn Crawl

In Tuscany, where wool, yarn and fabric have played such an important part in history, yarn shops are harder to find than hens' teeth, especially outside of the large cities. Yarn can be found in shops that carry notions, sewing supplies and even souvenirs. In the smaller towns this requires some exploration, but that's part of the fun. Try asking the locals for *negozi di filati* (yarn shops). In Florence I discovered four lovely shops that are worth your time seeking out. But fair warning, the yarns are extremely alluring—make sure you bring extra luggage to carry them home. I'm sad to report that after 40 years as the queen of Florence yarn shops, Beatrice Galli has closed the doors of her wonderful store. It was a favorite of mine and of visitors from around the world. She will be sorely missed, but you can visit these other shops to get your yarn fix.

1. Campolmi Roberto Filati (Via Folco Portinari 19/21r; campolmifilati.it) is by far the largest yarn shop in Florence. It sells a dizzying array of discounted yarns from Italy and around the world. The selection is so great, I felt like I was in yarn heaven when I was there. I bought some unusual wooden knitting needles that I used in designing pieces for this book. The staff is helpful and the shop is located in a lovely neighborhood not far from the Duomo. Plan on spending some time here.

2. Beaded Lily (Sdrucciolo dei Pitti 13r; beadedlily.com) is a fun and fabulously funky shop just down a side street from the Palazzo Pitti. It has been run by American designer Lily Mordà for over 20

years and carries a small but interesting cache of yarn, along with an amazing selection of handmade glass beads (many designed by her husband, Tim), beadmaking supplies, designer jewelry, unique pendants, Swarovski crystals, wiremesh ribbon and lots more great stuff. Lily, who comes to Florence by way of San Francisco, Seattle and Tucson, is as interesting as her shop. You're bound to walk out with a bag of goodies. I did!

3. Maglieria Merceria Filati (Via de' Cerchi 7r) is half yarn shop, half notions and clothing store. There is a nice selection of yarns at good prices, and the shop is just off the magnificent Piazza della Signoria, which you're bound to visit. The friendly proprietors speak just enough English to get you through the yarn-buying experience. Then stroll over to the piazza for a cappuccino, gelato or glass of vino and some fantastic people-watching.

4. Mirko Filati di Campi Antonella e Barbara (Piazza San Lorenzo 35r; mirkofilati.it) is a tiny yarn shop in the Piazza San Lorenzo right next to the magnificent Basilica di San Lorenzo (the Medici family church) containing works by Michelangelo, Donatello, Bronzino and others. You can fufill your artistic, religious, historical and yarn-hunting pursuits all in one compact area. We discovered this shop on our last evening in Florence, when it was closed, but the yarns in the window looked interesting. So give it a try and let me know how it is. ●

A Visit to the Luigi Boldrini Yarn Mill

Italian yarn and fabric mills are famous the world over for the quality of their products. Their claim to fame in the fashion and knitting world is undisputed. This is where what you will be knitting and what you will be wearing begins. The mills are not open to the general public, but through the good graces of Alan Getz (JCA/Reynolds), a friend and sometimes employer, and his charming, knowledgeable Tuscan contact, Piero Gualandrini, I gained access to one of the most prestigious manufacturing and design mills in Italy: Luigi Boldrini Chenille and Fancy Yarns (luigiboldrini.com). It's located just on the outskirts of Florence. Luigi Boldrini is known as "the father of chenille," and the firm produces not only the finest chenille, but many other high-end fibers and microfibers. They supply these superior fibers to the crème de la crème of designers, manufacturers and knitting yarn companies throughout the world.

Piero had managed to get me in between the Donna Karan and Ralph Lauren appointments (pardon the name-dropping), and I was ushered into the office of the head man, Roberto Boldrini (one of Luigi's two sons), who gave us some of the history of the firm. Luigi Boldrini had built a machine for the production of chenille yarn, but it was destroyed by bombs during World War II. In 1946, Luigi rebuilt the machine from memory with whatever spare parts were available in postwar Italy and started his business. His sons Roberto and Giuliano came into the business and designed and built the first direct-feed chenille machine, which became the prototype for all the modern chenille machines used today. Illustrations and photographs of early machines line the walls of Roberto's office. We asked if we could see the current machinery, but our request was politely denied with the explanation that this is where the "magic" process happens, and it is top-secret. (I wondered whether Donna and Ralph were allowed to see it, but I don't think so.)

Roberto took us into the fabulous showroom/workroom to meet a third-generation Boldrini, Tommaso, who kindly continued our education.

This is where knitting trends get started. The room was filled with fabulous yarns and wonderful scarves and shawls created by designers for display to the Laurens, Karans, Guccis, Puccis, Diors, Versaces, Wangs and Epsteins.

Tommaso explained that the mill will design pieces for designers or take design or color suggestions from name designers and create the yarn or fabrics on their machines to their specifications. The creativity is in the machinery, and the speed and subtle setting of the angles of the machines determine the texture, patterns and even the colors of the yarn. The same thread going through the machine can change color with the slightest adjustment, and the Boldrinis are masters of the process. Tommaso showed us some of the new yarns, including a black-and-silver sparkle yarn that was absolutely elegant. He said most of the wool, cotton and synthetics had been coming from Austria and Germany, but China was rapidly becoming a major supplier (something that we heard in a number of places). The Boldrinis were wonderful and took their time showing me around, making me feel very special. And then, to top it off, Piero took us to lunch for a big plate of *pici,* a regional pasta of Tuscany, in a delectable red sauce. ●

Vecchio (Via Por Santa Maria/Via Guicciardini), which means "old bridge," is Florence's oldest (1345) and most famous bridge. Spanning the Arno River, it is an icon of the city. It originally housed butchers and residences but is now filled with tourists, souvenir vendors and jewelry stores (no real bargains but great fun). It should be on your "don't miss" list. **Piazza della Signoria,** a beautiful and lively piazza with the Palazzo Vecchio, the Fountain of Neptune, a statue of Grand Duke Cosimo on horseback, reproductions of famous statues (including the *David*) and fascinating people-watching, is a tourist mecca. After you've walked around it, sit down for a rest and a coffee at one of the cafés and enjoy the show.

SHOPPING

If you've got any euros left after visiting our four yarn shops (see page 19), you'll find shopping in Florence can be fun, whether it's for schlock or chic. The **Mercato di San Lorenzo** (Via dell'Ariento) is a hectic outdoor flea market around the streets of the Piazza San Lorenzo that sells souvenirs, T-shirts, designer knock-offs, silk scarves and low- to high-quality leather garments (I got a lovely suede cape). Don't be afraid to haggle over the price of everything; it is not only expected but encouraged. *Warning: Pickpockets thrive here, so protect your valuables.* The indoor **Mercato Centrale** here sells all kinds of foods for a quick lunch or a picnic. It's great fun! You'll find your Guccis, Armanis, etc. on streets like **Via de' Tornabuoni** and **Villa della Vigna Nuova,** but no great bargains. A really good variety of shopping (and gelato) can be found along the **Via Calzaiuoli,** which runs from the Duomo to the Piazza della Signoria. Peek into the charming Piazza della Repubblica along the way and visit **La Rinascente** department store. One of the most interesting shopping streets is **Borgo San Jacopo,** with clothing, jewelry, antique and other unique shops. Some of the best: **A Piedi Nudi nel Parco** (#38r; apiedinudinelparco.com) with one-of-a-kind women's, men's and children's clothing, accessories, textiles, perfumes and gorgeous sweaters. They helped me lighten my load of euros. **Angela Caputi** (#44/46; angelacaputi.com) carries an outrageously beautiful and unusual selection of glass and plastic jewelry, much of which comes in big, bold colors and sizes. **Obsequium** (#17/39) is an impressive wine shop. A few more shops: **Viadelcorso** (Via del Corso 28) is a really fun gift and novelty shop. **Enzo and Renato Rafanelli** (Via del Sol 13) has one of the greatest collection of knockers (brass door knockers, that is) that I have ever seen. Another wonderful shop nearby is **Arti e Mestieri** (Borgo degli Albizi 67r; artiemestieri.it), which sells Tuscan-style arts and crafts. And last, but not least, you must visit the **Maestro d'Arte Spitaletta Cameo Factory** (Via Borgo S.S. Apostoli 4). This is far from a "factory"; rather, it's a wonderful little shop where young men still carry on the dying art of hand-carving cameos. The selection runs from classical to contemporary designs, and you can watch the art being practiced before your eyes.

Well, that's my Firenze. Live it, love it, knit it! ●

Favorite son of Florence
I created a wool version of Carlo Collodi's famous literary creation. Here it is shown unfelted. The felted version is shown on page 33.

Dante's Beatrice Shawl

Dante's muse (and unrequited love of his life) was my inspiration for this elegant seed stitch shawl with sinuous cord appliqué and feather trim.

SIZE
Approx 12"W x 65"L/30.5 x 165cm

MATERIALS
❖ 10 50g balls (each approx 110yds/99m) of Trendsetter Yarns *Kashmir*, 65% cashmere/35% silk, in #26976 charcoal

❖ 90"/229cm of Trendsetter Yarns *Boa* (ostrich feathers/goose down) in haze

❖ Size 10 (6mm) needles, OR SIZE TO OBTAIN GAUGE

❖ Size 6 (4mm) double-pointed needles

❖ Sewing needle and matching thread

GAUGE
17 sts and 27 rows = 4"/10cm in Seed st
TAKE TIME TO CHECK GAUGE

SEED ST (over an odd number of stitches)
Row 1 K1, *p1, k1; rep from * to end.
Rep row 1 for patt.

SCARF
With larger needles, cast on 37 sts.
Work in Seed st, inc 1 st at beg of each row until there are 51 sts, incorporating new sts into patt. Work even in Seed st until piece measures 63"/160cm.

Dec 1 st at beg of each row until 37 sts rem. Bind off in patt.

Position boa around perimeter of scarf and sew in place using needle and thread.

CORSET LACE APPLIQUE
With dpns, cast on 4 sts. Work 4 I-cords (see page 111) each 46"/117cm in length.

Using diagram as guide for placement, sew cords to RS of shawl at either end. ●

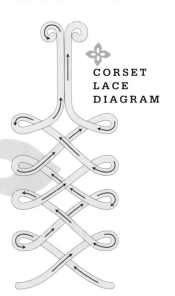

CORSET LACE DIAGRAM

Wool Guild Wreath

This knit wreath is based on Andrea della Robbia's glazed terra-cotta coat of arms for the prestigious Wool Guild. On your wall it declares your affiliation with the International Order of Knitters.

SIZE
Approx 16–18"/40.5-45.5cm diameter

MATERIALS
❖ 3 100g hanks (each approx 137 yds/123m) of Manos del Uruguay/Fairmount Fibers, Ltd. *Wool*, 100% wool, in #65 wheat (A)

❖ 1 skein each in #E english (B), #29 steel (C), #Z straw (D), #X topaz (E), #28 copper (F), #43 juniper (G), #14 natural (H), #M bing cherry (I) and #D spruce (J)

❖ Size 11 (8mm) needles, OR SIZE TO OBTAIN GAUGE

❖ Size 10 (6mm) double-pointed needles

❖ Quilt batting

❖ Polyester fiberfill

❖ Tapestry needle

❖ Hot glue gun and fabric glue sticks (optional)

GAUGE
12 sts and 16 rows = 4"/10cm in St st on larger needles, before felting
TAKE TIME TO CHECK GAUGE

CENTER MEDALLION
With G, cast on 39 sts.
Work 83 rows of Chart in St st. Bind off. Make French knots (see page 111) in charted area; embroider flagpole and accents on flag using Stem stitch (see page 111); and embroider fleur de lis in each segment along top border of chart. Add eyes, nose and mouth in Duplicate stitch (see page 111), using photo as guide.

WREATH
With A, cast on 43 sts. Work in St st for 58"/147.5cm.

CORD BANDS
With dpns and E, cast on 4 sts. Work I-cord (see page 111) for approx 3 yds/2.75m.

APPLES (make 8)

With D, cast on 12 sts, leaving a long tail for seaming.
Row 1 (RS) *Kfb; rep from * to end—24 sts.
Rows 2, 4, 6, 8, 10, 12 and 14 Purl.
Rows 3, 5, 7, 9, 11 and 13 Knit.
Row 15 *K2tog; rep from * to end—12 sts.
Change to E.
Row 16 *P2tog; rep from * to end—6 sts.
Row 17 *K2tog; rep from * to end—3 sts.
Row 18 P3tog—1 st.
Fasten off. Thread tail through cast-on sts, gather and secure. Stuff lightly with fiberfill and sew side seam.

GRAPES (make 4)

MB (make bobble) K in front, back, front, back and front of st, turn. P5, turn; k5, turn; pass 2nd, 3rd, 4th and 5th sts over first st.
With I, cast on 13 sts.
Row 1 (RS) Knit.
Row 2 Purl.
Row 3 *K1, MB; rep from *, end k1.
Row 4 P2tog, p to last 2 sts, p2tog—11 sts.
Rows 5–12 Rep rows 3 and 4—3 sts after row 12.
Row 13 Sk2p—1 st.
Fasten off.
After felting, cut each bunch in half vertically.

PINECONES (make 6)

With E, cast on 24 sts.
Rows 1 and 3 (RS) Purl.
Row 2 *[K1, p1, k1] in next st, p3tog; rep from * to end.
Row 4 *P3tog, [k1, p1, k1] in next st; rep from * to end.
Rows 5–12 Rep rows 1–4.
Rows 13 and 14 Rep rows 1 and 2.
Row 15 *K2tog, p2tog; rep from * to end—12 sts.
Row 16 *K2tog; rep from * to end—6 sts.
Row 17 *P2tog; rep from * to end—3 sts.

Row 18 Sk2p—1 st.
Fasten off, leaving a 12"/30.5cm tail. Thread tail through cast-on sts, gather and secure. Stuff lightly with fiberfill and sew side seam.

GRAPE LEAF (make 3)

With C, cast on 5 sts.
Row 1 (RS) *K1, M1; rep from *, end k1—9 sts.
Rows 2, 4, and 6 Purl.
Row 3 *K1, M1; rep from *, end k1—17 sts.
Row 5 Knit.
Row 7 Bind off 3 sts, k to end—14 sts.
Row 8 Bind off 3 sts, p to end—11 sts.
Row 9 Rep row 1—21 sts.
Rows 10 and 12 Purl.
Row 11 Knit.
Row 13 Bind off 4 sts, k to end—17 sts.
Row 14 Bind off 4 sts, p to end—13 sts.
Row 15 K5, sk2p, k5—11 sts.
Rows 16, 18, 20, 22 and 24 Purl.
Row 17 K4, sk2p, k4—9 sts.
Row 19 K3, sk2p, k3—7 sts.
Row 21 K2, sk2p, k2—5 sts.
Row 23 K1, sk2p, k1—3 sts.
Row 25 Sk2p—1 st.
Fasten off.
With D, embroider veins onto leaves using Stem st.

TECHNIQUE
Felting Basics

1 Fill washing machine to low water setting at a hot temperature. Add 1/2 cup of gentle detergent.
2 Add all pieces (may be placed in a lingerie bag or pillowcase) and a pair of jeans to provide abrasion and balanced agitation.
3 Use 15–20 minute wash cycle, including cold rinse and spin. Repeat process until desired felting effect is achieved.
4 Lay flat to dry.

CENTER MEDALLION

83
80
70
60
50
40
30
20
10
1

39 STITCHES

Stitch Key

⊠ K2tog
⊠ Ssk
⊠ Kfb
○ French Knot with H
╲ Stem Stitch with H

Color Key

■ COPPER (F)
▨ JUNIPER (G)
□ NATURAL (H)

FAN LEAF (make 5)
With J, cast on 19 sts.
Row 1 and all WS rows Purl.
Row 2 K1, *yo, k2, ssk, k2tog, k2, yo, k1;
rep from * to end.
Row 4 K3, ssk, k2tog, k2, yo, k1, yo, k2, ssk,
k2tog, k3— 17 sts.
Row 6 K2, ssk, k2tog, k2, yo, k1, yo, k2, ssk,
k2tog, k2—15 sts.
Row 8 K1, ssk, k2tog, k2, yo, k1, yo, k2, ssk,
k2tog, k1—13 sts.
Row 10 K5, sk2p, k5—11 sts.
Row 12 K4, sk2p, k4—9 sts.
Row 14 K3, sk2p, k3—7 sts.
Row 16 K2, sk2p, k2—5 sts.
Row 18 K1, sk2p, k1—3 sts.
Row 20 Sk2p—1 st.
Fasten off.
With G, embroider veins onto leaves
using Stem st.

PETAL LEAF (make 10)
With J, cast on 3 sts.
Row 1 and all WS rows Purl.
Rows 2, 4 and 6 Kfb, k to last st, kfb—9 sts
after row 6.
Rows 8, 10, 12 and 14 Knit.
Rows 16, 18 and 20 Ssk, k to last 2 sts,
k2tog—3 sts after row 20.
Row 22 Sk2p—1 st.
Fasten off.
With D, embroider veins onto leaves
using Stem st.

APPLE LEAF
(make 23 assorted with B, C and J)
Cast on 5 sts.
Row 1 (RS) K2, yo, k1, yo, k2—7 sts.
Rows 2, 4, 6, 8, 10 and 12 Purl.
Row 3 K3, yo, k1, yo, k3—9 sts.
Row 5 K4, yo, k1, yo, k4—11 sts.
Row 7 Knit.

Rows 8, 10, 12 and 14 Purl.
Rows 9, 11, 13 and 15 Ssk, k to last 2 sts,
k2tog—3 sts after row 15.
Row 16 P3tog—1 st.
Fasten off.
With D, embroider accents onto J leaves using
Duplicate st (see page 111).

LEAF TRIPLET (MAKE 3)

With dpns and E, cast on 3 sts. Work I-cord
for 3"/7.5cm.
Next row Pfb, p1, pfb—5 sts.
Work rows 1–16 of apple leaf.
With E, work 2 more apple leaves and sew to
cord at each side of first leaf.
With D, embroider accents onto one triplet
using duplicate st.

FINISHING

Felt all pieces (see page 26).
Cut quilt batting to length and roll tightly to fit
into wreath. Baste with sewing thread to secure
its shape. Place felted wreath strip around batting
and sew back seam, then sew end seam to form
a ring. Cut cord into 8 pieces, wrap around
wreath, spacing evenly, and sew in place. Sew
or use a hot glue gun to attach appliques to
wreath, using photo as guide. Sew center
medallion onto back of wreath. Cut a cardboard
circle to fit back of wreath and use fabric glue
or hot glue gun to secure. ●

Wreath

Pinecone

Leaf triplet

*Embroidered
apple leaf*

Apple

Cord band

Grape leaf

Grapes

Petal leaf

Center medallion

Apple leaf

Fan leaf

Medici Scarf

The Medici family's patronage was the most influential force in the Renaissance, and this extra-long scarf knit in royal colors pays homage to their dedication to the arts.

SIZE
7"W x 80"L/17.5 x 203cm

MATERIALS
❖ 1 50g ball (each approx 61yds/55m) of Muench Yarns *Touch Me*, 72% rayon microfiber/28% wool, each in #3619 chocolate (A), #3646 purple (B), #3652 dark rust (C), #3603 dark teal (D), #3615 gold (E), #3602 grape (F), #3610 olive (G) and #3851 rust (H)

❖ Size 7 (4.5mm) needles
OR SIZE TO OBTAIN GAUGE

❖ Tapestry needle

❖ Polyester fiberfill

GAUGE
16 sts and 20 rows =
4"/10cm in St st
TAKE TIME TO CHECK GAUGE

SCARF
With A, cast on 29 sts.
Row 1 (RS) *K5, p1; rep from *, end k5.
Row 2 *P5, k1; rep from *, end p5.
Rep rows 1 and 2 for 10"/25.5cm, end with a WS row.
*Change to B and rep rows 1 and 2 for 10"/25.5cm. Rep from * with colors C, D, E, F, G and H.
Bind off.

BALLS
(make 16 in various colors)
Cast on 8 sts, leaving a long tail for sewing.
Row 1 (RS) *Kfb; rep from * to end—16 sts.
Row 2 and all WS rows Purl.
Rows 3, 5, 7 and 9 Knit.
Row 11 *K2tog, rep from * to end—8 sts.
Cut yarn, leaving a long tail. Thread tail through rem sts, draw tight and secure. Thread cast-on tail through cast-on sts, draw tight and secure. Stuff with fiberfill and sew side seam. Using tails, sew to RS of scarf as pictured. ●

✤ *Round and round*
The balls are knit separately, stuffed lightly with polyester fiberfill and attached at random.

Pinocchio

Florence-born author Carlo Collodi created the world's most loveable liar. My version is wool, not wood, and I hope it serves as an example to your favorite child to never lie...unless absolutely necessary!

SIZE
Approx 28" H/71cm, before felting
Approx 24" H/61cm, after felting

MATERIALS
❖ 1 100g hank (each approx 220yds/198m) of Cascade Yarns *Cascade 220*, 100% Peruvian highland wool, each in #8021 tan (A), #9430 green (B), #9404 red (C) and small amount #8555 black (D)

❖ Size 9 (5.5mm) needles, OR SIZE TO OBTAIN GAUGE

❖ Size 6 (4mm) double-pointed needles

❖ Stitch holder

❖ Tapestry needle

❖ Three ¾" black buttons

❖ 1 bag polyester fiberfill

❖ Sharp pt. sewing needle

❖ Permanent marker in light pink

❖ Feather (optional)

GAUGE
18 sts and 24 rows = 4"/10cm in St st on larger needles, before felting
TAKE TIME TO CHECK GAUGE

BODY (make 2)

Legs
Starting at the ankle with A and larger needles, cast on 21 sts. Work in St st for 6½"/16.5cm, end with a WS row.
Inc row (RS) Kfb, k to last st, kfb.
Cont in St st, rep inc row every 8th row 4 times more—31 sts.

Pants
Change to B. Cont in St st, rep inc row every 4th row 3 times—37 sts.
Work even until B section measures 3"/7.5cm.
Bind off 4 sts at beg of next 2 rows, then dec 1 st at beg of foll 4 rows—25 sts.
Work even for 2"/5cm.

Torso
Change to C. Cont even in St st for 5"/12.5cm, end with a WS row.
Dec row (RS) K to center 3 sts, sk2p, k to end.
P 1 row.
Rep last 2 rows 3 times more—17 sts.
Place sts on holder.

Make 2nd piece; do not cut yarn and leave sts on needle.
Sew inner legs, leaving a 2"/5cm opening below start of inc. Sew front body seam.

❖ *Note*
Pinocchio's body is knit in 2 halves.

BEFORE FELTING

Neck

Work across sts on needle then sts from holder—34 sts.

Dec row (RS) *K1, k2tog; rep from *,
end k1—23 sts.

Change to A and p 1 row; k 1 row; p 1 row.

Dec row (RS) *K1, k2tog; rep from *,
end k2—16 sts.

Work 5 rows in St st.

HEAD

Inc row (RS) *Kfb; rep from * to end—32 sts.
P 1 row.

Rep last 2 rows—64 sts.

Work even in St st for 4"/10cm,
end with a WS row.

Dec row (RS) *K2tog; rep from * to end—32 sts.
P 1 row.

Rep last 2 rows once—16 sts.

Rep dec row once more—8 sts.

Cut yarn, leaving a 12"/30.5cm tail. Thread tail through rem sts, draw tight and secure. Sew back of head seam, leaving a 2"/5cm opening. Sew back body seam, leaving a 3"/7.5 cm opening.

HANDS/ARMS (make 2)

With A and larger needles, cast on 5 sts.

Row 1 *Kfb; rep from * to end—10 sts.

Row 2 Purl.

Row 3 *K1, kfb; rep from * to end—15 sts.

Cont in St st, inc 1 st each side every 6th row 4 times—23 sts.

Work even until piece measures 5½"/14cm
from beg, end with a WS row.

Change to C, work in St st for 6 rows.

Inc row (RS) *K1, kfb; rep from *,
end k1—34 sts.

Work even in St st for 2"/5cm, end with a WS row.

Dec row (RS) *K2tog; rep from * to end—17 sts.

P 1 row. Bind off.

Sew arm seams, leaving a 2"/5cm opening in C section.

SHOES (make 2)

With D and and larger needles, cast on 5 sts.

Row 1 *Kfb; rep from * to end—10 sts.

Row 2 Purl.

Rep last 2 rows once—20 sts.

Work even in St st until piece measures
4"/10cm from beg.

Divide sts evenly over 2 needles and with RS tog, work 3-needle bind-off (see page 111).

Starting from toe, sew top seam, leaving 2"/5cm opening for leg.

HAT (make 2)

With C and larger needles, cast on 31 sts.

Work in St st for 2"/5cm, end with a WS row.

Dec row (RS) K1, k2 tog, k to last 3 sts, ssk, k1.
P 1 row.

Rep last 2 rows until 5 sts rem.

Next row K1, s2kp, k1—3 sts. Bind off.

Sew side seams, reversing seam at bottom for rolled hem.

Hatband

With B and dpns, cast on 5 sts. Work I-cord (see page 111) for 13"/33cm. Bind off.

HAIR

With D and larger needles, *cast on 9 sts, bind off 8 sts, slip rem st to left-hand needle; rep from * 8 more times for 9 fringes.
Fasten off.

COLLAR

With C and larger needles, cast on 61 sts.

K 3 rows. Work in St st for 1"/2.5cm, beg and end with a p row.

He's such a nose-it-all!

Your Pinocchio's nose length can be adjusted according to how many lies you've told.

Dec row (RS) K1, *k2tog; rep from * across row—31 sts.
Next row P1, *k1, p1; rep from * to end. Cont in rib for ½"/1.25cm. Bind off.

PEPLUM
With C and larger needles, cast on 79 sts. K 3 rows. Work in St st for 2"/5cm, beg and end with a p row.
Dec row (RS) *K1, k2tog; rep from *, end k1—53 sts.
Next row P1, *k1, p1; rep from * to end. Cont in rib for ½"/1.25cm. Bind off.

NOSE
With A and dpns, cast on 5 sts. Work I-cord (see page 111) for 5"/12.5cm. Bind off.

BOWTIE
Bow
With B and larger needles, cast on 7 sts.
Next row *K1, p1; rep from *, end k1. Cont in rib for 2¼"/1.5cm. Bind off.

Tie
With B and larger needles, cast on 5 sts, bind off 5 sts. Place tie around center and stitch in place.

FINISHING
Sew one shoe onto each leg. With D, embroider eyes using short and long straight sts.
With C, work mouth in stem st. Sew hair and nose in place. Sew hat to head, leaving a 4" back opening. Sew hatband to hat. Sew arms to shoulders. Sew collar and bowtie to neck. Sew peplum to waist.
Felt Pinnochio (see page 26). Stuff while slightly damp and sew closed all openings. Let dry completely. With permanent pink marker, make circles on cheeks (see photo). Sew on buttons. Add feather to hat.●

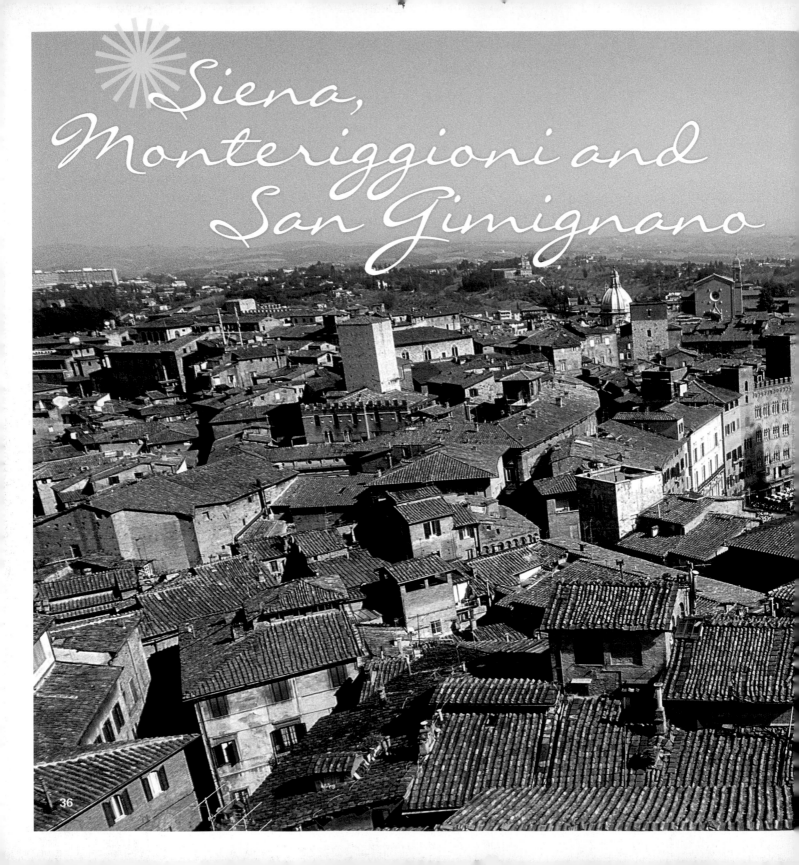

Siena, Monteriggioni and San Gimignano

✤ Up on a Tuscan Roof
The magnificent Piazza del Campo is the heart of Siena.

SIENA, a medieval city of brick sitting atop three hills, is arguably the most beautiful city in Tuscany. Siena flourished over the centuries with the aid of the successful Wool Traders Guild (no wonder we love Italian wool) and was a longtime rival of Florence. Just walking its romantic, hilly streets filled with ancient multicolored buildings, palaces, pastry shops and museums holding treasures of Sienese art (to say nothing of the three yarn shops that we found) can be the highlight of a trip to Tuscany.

ACCOMODATIONS

Hotel Antica Torre (Via di Fiera Vecchia 7; anticatorresiena.it) features eight simple but lovely guest rooms in a sixteenth-century tower. **Hotel Duomo** (Via Stalloreggi 38; hotelduomo.it) has pleasant rooms in a twelfth-century palazzo located between the Duomo and the Piazza del Campo. Some rooms have views of the Duomo, and the brick-walled breakfast room is a nice place to start the day. **Palazzo Ravizza** (Pian dei Mantellini 34; palazzoravizza.it) is a ten-minute walk from the Duomo. You'll find rooms with high ceilings, antique furnishings and tiled bathrooms. It has a pleasant feeling of faded elegance.

DINING

Osteria le Logge (Via del Porrione 33) is a beautiful restaurant just off the Piazza del Campo. Its changing menu includes dishes like duck baked with grapes, ravioli stuffed with sheep's-milk cheese, pasta with truffle sauce and exceptional desserts. **Osteria del Coro** (Via Pantaneto 85; osteriadelcoro.it) has a subdued décor and super food. Try the old Sienese dish *pici con le briciole* (thick spaghetti with bread crumbs and bacon—wow!). Look for more restaurants a block up from the Campo on the perimeter streets Via di Città and Via Banchi di Sotto. If the restaurants are filled with locals, join them!

SIGHTSEEING

The incredible **Piazza del Campo** is the center of Siena. This is the most lovely and lively square in Tuscany and is filled with tourists and locals alike sitting at cafés, gelaterias and restaurants that ring this shell-shaped, sloping plaza. Here, along with many beautiful medieval buildings, you'll find the **Palazzo Pubblico,** the impressive Gothic town hall with its 335-foot-tall bell tower, the **Torre del Mangia,** which is the most recognizable and dominant structure of the Siena skyline. Visit the **Museo Civico** (Civic Museum), which is filled with Sienese masterpieces and wonderful Lorenzetti frescoes. You can also just sit in the piazza for hours and not be bored for an instant. With its colored bands of marble, Siena's incredible cathedral, the **Duomo,** seems to glow like something out of a dream. It has a spectacular Tuscan Gothic façade, but its black-and-white-striped interior is just as impressive. The floor itself is made up of works of art, and in a small chapel in a glass box is a human arm that is said to be the right arm of John the Baptist, which he used to baptize Christ. The whole experience is mystical.

On July 2 and August 16 the Piazza del Campo is the scene of the most famous festival/horse race in Italy: the **Palio delle Contrade.** Riders from Siena's *contrade* (neighborhoods) sport their colors and flags and compete in a wild and woolly race around the Campo. Thousands of people pack the piazza to witness this 90-second, no-holds-barred race (riders and horses have been known to go flying). Prior to the race there are parades and pageantry, with locals wearing handmade medieval costumes and a spectacular exhibition of flag-throwing. The winning *contrada* celebrates all night (and even longer) with a banquet and festivities. The Palio is great fun, but not for the fainthearted or the claustrophobic.

SIENA

Siena Yarn Crawl

Located on a lovely sloping street, **Casa della Lana** (Via delle Terme 59) is run by a husband-and-wife team and carries lots of yarn at very nice prices. I had a great time diving into a line of beautiful and unusual buttons. **Cose di Lana** (Via Pantaneto 17) is a small shop with a good-sized collection of fine yarns. **Il Filo di Arianna** (Via Cavour Camillo Benso 78) is a charming shop that sits just outside the city center but is worth the effort it takes to get there.

SHOPPING IN SIENA

There are all kinds of shops along the aforementioned **Via di Città** and **Via Banchi di Sotto,** as well as on many streets that run from the city walls to the Piazza del Campo. **Martini Marisa** (Via del Capitano 5/11; anticasiena.it) and **Antica Siena** (Piazza del Campo 28; anticasiena.it) are two shops that sell colorful and beautiful ceramics and handmade pottery. (They ship, so you can keep all that extra room in your luggage for yarn.) At **Tessuti a Mano** (Via San Pietro 7), Fioretta Baci weaves incredible sweaters and jackets of wool, mohair, silk, linen and cotton on the premises. Candy, pastries, cookies and cakes are everywhere in Siena, but one of the best places to get them is **Caffè Nannini** (Via Massetana Romana 56; caffenannini.it). You can purchase Sienese specialties like a fabulous *panforte* (including a chocolate one) and *ricciarelli* (almond cookies), which you can take back home to share with friends (or just make them jealous).

Taking a break

My top three travel tips: Wear comfortable shoes, wear comfortable shoes, wear comfortable shoes.

MONTERIGGIONI is the perfect small medieval village. The thirteenth-century walls and buildings are among the best preserved in all of Tuscany. As you approach the town from a distance, it looks like a picture postcard, and when you enter the gates to the city (there is plenty of parking just outside the walls), it's like walking back in time. I love Monteriggioni!

ACCOMODATIONS

Hotel Monteriggioni (Via 1 Maggio 4; hotelmonteriggioni.net) has twelve comfortable rooms, and the atmosphere is that of staying in a private home. There's a garden and a pool, and you can find tons of parking just outside the walls. **Hotel Il Piccolo Castello** (Via Colligiana 8; ilpiccolocastello.com) is a classy, more contemporary hotel with spacious rooms, private baths and a private garden and pool. The rooms are decorated in a neoclassic Sienese style, and there is a restaurant in the hotel, which is located less than a mile from Monteriggioni.

DINING

At the top of the square is one of my favorite restaurants in all of Italy, **Il Pozzo** (Piazza Roma 2; ilpozzo.net). Dine in the beautiful restaurant or in the lovely back garden. The service is friendly, and the large menu features classic Tuscan dishes like fried zucchini blossoms (amazing), ravioli with truffles, *pici* with wild boar sauce, roast squab, walnut tart and heavenly Tuscan wines.

SIGHTSEEING

The beautiful **Piazza Roma** is surrounded by charming shops, cafés, restaurants, stunning buildings and the church of **Santa Maria Assunta.**

San Gimignano

Monteriggioni can be walked in ten minutes, but take your time and savor this Tuscan gem.

SHOPPING IN MONTERIGGIONI

Near the souvenir shops on Piazza Roma, you'll find two wonderful shops. **I Toscanacci Boutique** (Via 1 Maggio 15) sells fine men's and women's clothing and the most beautiful handmade straw hats I've ever seen. **Mobili d'Arte Antica** (Via 1 Maggio 17/18) carries a wonderful selection of antiques, including an incredible clock collection.

SAN GIMIGNANO,

Tuscany's most medieval city, is known as the "Medieval Manhattan" because of its impressive towers that rise up like skyscapers. The towers were built to help defend the city and as symbols of their owners' wealth. Fourteen of the original 70-plus towers still stand, giving the city its unique look and attracting many tourists. San Gimignano can be a busy town, but sitting in a piazza watching swallows fly around the stately towers as the sun sets is a heavenly experience.

ACCOMODATIONS

My favorite hotel in the heart of town is the **Hotel L'Antico Pozzo** (Via San Matteo 87; anticopozzo.com), a fifteenth-century *palazzo* that was converted to a hotel in 1990. My good-sized room had beautiful frescoes on the walls and ceiling, and the breakfast room was elegant. Parking is not allowed in the town center, so you have to park outside the walls—about a 10- to 15-minute walk back to the hotel, but it's a nice walk.

DINING

The best meal in town can be had at the **Ristorante Le Terrazze** (Piazza della Cisterna 23; hotelcistern.it), which is located in the Hotel Cisterna. The food, service and views of the surrounding countryside are stunning. For dessert we had the best *cantucci* and *vin santo* in Tuscany.

SIGHTSEEING

In the center of the city is the **Piazza del Duomo,** where you'll find the town's main church, the **Collegiata,** which is jam-packed with amazing fourteenth-century frescoes. Behind the piazza is the **Rocca Fortress;** climb its ramparts for unparalleled views of the surrounding farmland and the jutting town towers. Also located in the Piazza del Duomo is the **Museo Civico,** which features Pinturicchio's *Madonna* and provocative frescoes by Filipucci.

SHOPPING

San Gimignano is a very touristy town with lots of varied shopping on **Via San Giovanni** and **Via San Matteo.** Look for yarn along the way. ●

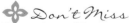 *Don't Miss*

No grand tour of Tuscany would be complete without visits to **Pisa,** with its impressive askew monument to poor planning (the Leaning Tower), and **Lucca,** a beautiful walled Renaissance city in northern Tuscany.

DAY TRIP
Volterra

Located only 18 miles from San Gimignano, Volterra makes a fascinating day trip. The city is rich with Etruscan art, including beautiful bronzes and all kinds of alabaster carvings and decorations. Volterra is called "Alabaster City," and modern artists here still work in alabaster. See the **Piazza dei Priori** in the middle of the city, but leave enough time for a long visit to the **Museo Etrusco Guarnacci** (Via Don Minzoni 15). It is one of the finest Etruscan museums in Italy and has an incredible collection of artifacts, including over 600 funerary urns. The **Roman Theater and Baths** date from the first century B.C. and are among the best-preserved ruins in Italy.

We saw a glorious sunset from the heights of Volterra, and on the way back to San Gimignano a wild boar almost collided with our car. He was probably angry at us for eating all that *cinghiale!* ●

Dining delight
The lovely Il Pozzo restaurant in Monteriggioni is one of my favorite restaurants in all of Italy. Yummy!

Medieval Monteriggioni Festival

If you are lucky enough to be in Monteriggioni in July, you should not miss the **Medieval Monteriggioni Festival**, held on two three-day weekends. Hundreds of people from the surrounding area don eye-catching medieval costumes and really get into the spirit of things. Tourists are encouraged to join in. The festivities go on day and night, with realistic reenactments of battles, dancers (some on stilts), musicians, minstrels, pilgrims, peasants, noblemen, witches, beggars, monks, soldiers, jugglers, jesters, artisans, merchants and food, food, food, all deliciously cooked alfresco over grills. You'll never have a better day in Tuscany. ●

Siena Rooftop Sweater

The roofs of Siena are constructed with beautiful terra-cotta tiles.
This lovely sweater's design evokes their timelessness.

◼️◼️◻️◻️

SIZES
S (M, L, XL)
Finished bust 36 (40, 46, 50)"/91.5 (101.5, 117, 127)cm
Finished length 18½ (18½, 20½, 20½)"/47 (47, 52, 52)cm

MEASUREMENTS
Back width 18½ (20½, 23½, 25)"/46.5 (52, 60, 63.5)cm
Back length 18½ (18½, 20½, 20½)"/47 (47, 52, 52)cm
Neck width 10"/25.5cm
Shoulder width 4¼ (5¼, 6¾, 7½)"/10.5 (13.5, 17, 19)cm
Front width 9¼ (10¼, 11¾, 12½)"/23(26, 29, 32)cm
Sleeve cuff and upper arm width 16 (18¼, 19½, 20½)"/40.5 (46.5, 49.5, 52)cm
Sleeve length 10½"/26.5cm
Hood width 20½"/52cm
Hood length 12½"/32cm

MATERIALS
❖ 19 (21, 26, 28) 50g hanks (each approx 98yds/90m) of Berroco, Inc., *Jasper*, 100% fine merino wool, in #3840 brown santiago

❖ Size 9 (5.5mm) needles, OR SIZE TO OBTAIN GAUGE

❖ Tapestry needle

GAUGE
14 sts and 24 rows = 4"/10cm in staggered holster st
TAKE TIME TO CHECK GAUGE

STAGGERED HOLSTER ST
(multiple of 4 sts)
Row 1 (RS) P4, *turn, cast on 8 sts for holster, turn, p4; rep from * to end.
Row 2 K4, *p8, k4; rep from * to end.
Row 3 P4, *k8, p4; rep from * to end.
Rows 4–9 Rep rows 2 and 3.
Row 10 K4, *bind off 8 holster sts purlwise, k rem 3 sts; rep from * to end.
Row 11 Purl.
Row 12 Knit.
Row 13 P6, *turn, cast on 8 sts for holster, turn, p4; rep from * to last 2 sts, p2.
Row 14 K6, *p8, k4; rep from * to last 2 sts, k2.
Row 15 P6, *k8, p4; rep from * to last 2 sts, p2.
Rows 16–21 Rep rows 14 and 15.
Row 22 K6, *bind off 8 holster sts purlwise, k rem 3 sts; rep from * to last 2 sts, k2.
Row 23 Purl.
Row 24 Knit.
Rep rows 1–24 for pat.

BACK
Cast on 64 (72, 80, 88) sts. K 4 rows. Work rows 1–24 of Staggered Holster St 4 (4, 5, 5) times, then rows 1–12 once (once, 0, 0) more. Bind off.

LEFT FRONT
Cast on 32 (36, 40, 44) sts. Work same as Back.

RIGHT FRONT
Work same as Left Front.

SLEEVES

Cast on 56 (64, 68, 72) sts. K 4 rows. Work rows 1–24 of Staggered Holster St twice, then rows 1–12 once more. Bind off.

HOOD

Cast on 72 sts. K 4 rows. Work rows 1–24 of Staggered Holster St 3 times. Bind off.

FINISHING

Sew shoulder seams, leaving center 10"/25.5cm open for neck opening. Place markers at side seams, 8 (9, 9½, 10)"/20.5 (23, 24, 25.5)cm down from each shoulder. Set sleeves between markers and sew in. Sew side and sleeve seams. Fold hood in half widthwise and sew top seam. Sew hood to neck opening. ●

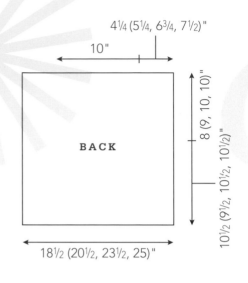

10"

4¼ (5¼, 6¾, 7½)"

8 (9, 10, 10)"

BACK

10½ (9½, 10½, 10½)"

18½ (20½, 23½, 25)"

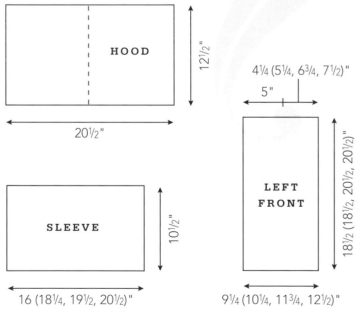

HOOD

12½"

20½"

SLEEVE

10½"

16 (18¼, 19½, 20½)"

4¼ (5¼, 6¾, 7½)"

5"

LEFT FRONT

18½ (18½, 20½, 20½)"

9¼ (10¼, 11¾, 12½)"

The stitch pattern and yarn color mimic the shape and colors of Sienese roof tiles.

Flower Power
From left to right: Pope's Poppy Pillow, Twist Fiore Pillow and Plumeria Pillow.

Della Robbia Flower Pillows

These gorgeous pillows adorned with knit flowers are inspired by Giovanni della Robbia's terra-cotta sculptures.

MATERIALS
- 3 100g hanks (each approx 193yds/173m) of Louet North America *Riverstone Light Worsted*, 100% wool, in #70 white (A)
- 1 hank each in #30 cream (B) and #1 champagne (C)
- Size 11 (8mm) needles, OR SIZE TO OBTAIN GAUGE
- Tapestry needle
- Small amount of polyester fiberfill
- Three 20"/51cm square pillows
- Hot glue gun and fabric glue sticks (optional)

GAUGE
Approx 12 sts and 18 rows = 4"/10cm in St st, before felting
TAKE TIME TO CHECK GAUGE
Lace leaf measures approx 3"W x 3¾"H/7.5 x 9.5cm, after felting

1 POPE'S POPPY PILLOW
LARGE PETAL
(make 20, 5 for each flower)
With A, cast on 3 sts.
Rows 1 and 7 (RS) Knit.
Row 2 and all WS rows Purl.
Rows 3 and 5 *K1, m1; rep from *, end k1—9 sts after row 5.
Row 9 *K1, m1; rep from *, end k1—17 sts.
Rows 11 and 13 *Ssk, k to last 2 sts, k2tog—13 sts after row 13.
Row 15 Ssk, bind off next 9 sts, k2tog and pass previous st over—1 st.
Fasten off.

SMALL PETAL
(make 12, 3 for each flower)
With A, cast on 3 sts.
Rows 1 and 7 (RS) Knit.
Row 2 and all WS rows Purl.
Rows 3 and 5 *K1, m1; rep from *, end k1—9 sts
after row 5.
Row 9 *K1, m1; rep from *, end k1—17 sts.
Row 11 Ssk, bind off 13 sts, k2tog
and pass previous st over—1 st.
Fasten off.

LACE LEAF (make 10)
With C, cast on 5 sts.
Row 1 (RS) K2, yo, k1, yo, k2—7 sts.
Row 2 and all WS rows Purl.
Row 3 K3, yo, k1, yo, k3—9 sts.
Row 5 K4, yo, k1, yo, k4—11 sts.
Row 7 K5, yo, k1, yo, k5—13 sts.
Rows 9, 11, 13, 15 and 17 Ssk, k to last 2 sts,
k2tog—3 sts after row 17.
Row 19 SK2P—1 st.
Fasten off.

ROSE (make 4)
With A, cast on 10 sts.
Row 1 (RS) Knit.
Row 2 and all WS rows Purl.
Rows 3, 5 and 7 *Kfb; rep from * to
end—80 sts after row 7.
Bind off.
Roll strip into a spiral, using tail to sew in place.●

2 TWIST FIORE PILLOW
TWIST FIORE (make 5)
With A, cast on 40 sts.
Rows 1–10 Knit.
Change to C.
Row 11 (RS) K2, *k5, rotate left-hand
needle counterclockwise 360 degrees;
rep from *, end k3.
Row 12 *P2tog; rep from * to end—20 sts.
Row 13 *K2tog; rep from * to end—10 sts.

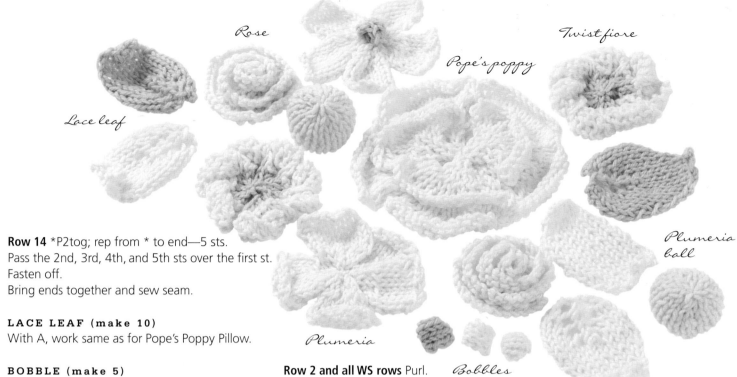

Rose

Lace leaf

Pope's poppy

Twist fiore

Plumeria
ball

Plumeria

Bobbles

Row 14 *P2tog; rep from * to end—5 sts.
Pass the 2nd, 3rd, 4th, and 5th sts over the first st.
Fasten off.
Bring ends together and sew seam.

LACE LEAF (make 10)
With A, work same as for Pope's Poppy Pillow.

BOBBLE (make 5)
With C, cast on 1 st.
Row 1 (RS) K in front, back, front, back,
front of st—5 sts.
Rows 2 and 4 Purl.
Row 3 and 5 Knit.
Pass the 2nd, 3rd, 4th and 5th sts over the first st.
Fasten off.●

3 PLUMERIA PILLOW
PETAL (make 35, 5 for each flower)
With A, cast on 3 sts.
Row 1 (RS) Kfb, k1, kfb—5 sts.
Row 2 and all WS rows Purl.
Row 3 *K1, m1; rep from *, end k1—9 sts.
Rows 5 and 7 Knit.
Rows 9 and 11 Ssk, k to last 2 sts, k2tog—5 sts
after row 11.
Bind off purlwise.

LEAF (make 9)
With A, cast on 3 sts.
Rows 1, 3 and 5 (RS) Kfb, k to last st, kfb—9 sts
after row 5.

Row 2 and all WS rows Purl.
Rows 7, 9, 11 and 13 Knit.
Rows 15, 17 and 19 Ssk, k to last
2 sts, k2tog—3 sts after row 19.
Row 21 SK2P—1 st.
Fasten off.

BALL (make 7)
With B, cast on 8 sts, leaving a long tail for sewing.
Row 1 (RS) *Kfb; rep from * to end—16 sts.
Row 2 and all WS rows Purl.
Rows 3, 5, 7 and 9 Knit.
Row 11 *K2tog, rep from * to end—8 sts.
Cut yarn, leaving a long tail. Thread tail through
rem sts, draw tight and secure. Thread cast-on
tail through cast-on sts, draw tight and secure.
Stuff lightly with fiberfill and sew side seam.
Bring tails to top and make 3 French knots (see
page 111) at center.

FINISHING
Felt pieces and let dry completely (see page 26)
Position petals and leaves as pictured. Sew or glue
into place. Sew or glue centers to each flower.●

San Gimignano

Fresco Vest

This vest celebrates the Etruscans, whose influence is found throughout Tuscany.

SIZES

S (M, L, XL); shown in M
Finished bust 40 (46½, 51, 57½)"/101.5 (118, 129.5, 146)cm
Finished length 26 (28, 28, 29)"/66 (71, 71, 71)cm

MEASUREMENTS

Lower edge width 17½ (21, 23¼, 26½)"/44.5 (53.5, 59, 67.5)cm
Chest width 20 (23¼, 25½, 28¾)"/51 (59, 65, 73)cm
Length to underarm 17 (18, 18, 18)"/43 (45.5, 45.5, 45.5)cm
Armhole depth 9 (10, 10, 11)"/23 (25.5, 25.5, 28)cm
V-neck depth 7"/18cm
Neck width 6¾"/17cm

MATERIALS

❖ 9 (10, 11, 13) 50g balls (each approx 138yds/125m) of GGH/Muench Yarns *Wollywasch*, 100% superwash wool, in #172 gold (A)

❖1 ball each in #97 pink (B), #130 burgundy (C), #166 blue (D), #129 chocolate (E), #169 tan (F), #124 green (G), #173 olive (H), #81 yellow (I) and #22 black (J)

❖ Size 6 (4mm) 16" circular needle

❖ Size 7 (4.5mm) needles, OR SIZE TO OBTAIN GAUGE

❖ Size 5 (3.75mm) double-pointed needles

GAUGE

20 sts and 28 rows = 4"/10cm in St st using largest size needles

FRONT

With smaller needles and A, cast on 88 (104, 116, 132) sts.
Row 1 (WS) P3, *k2, p2; rep from *, end p1.
Row 2 K3, *p2, k2; rep from *, end k1.
Rep rows 1 and 2 for 1½"/3.75cm. Change to larger needles and work in St st until piece measures 5½"/14cm from beg. Cont in St st, inc 1 st each side of next 3 RS rows—94 (110, 122, 138) sts. Cast on 3 sts at beg of next 2 rows—100 (116, 128, 144) sts. Cont even in St st until piece measures 17 (18, 18, 18)"/43 (45.5, 45.5, 45.5) cm from beg.

ARMHOLE SHAPING

Bind off 4 (5, 6, 8) sts at beg of next 2 rows, then dec 1 st each side every RS row 3 (3, 5, 5) times—86 (100, 106, 118) sts. Work even in St st until armhole measures 2 (3, 3, 4)"/5 (7.5, 7.5, 10)cm, end with a WS row.

NECK SHAPING

Dividing row (RS) K40 (47, 50, 56), join 2nd ball of yarn and bind off next 6 sts, k to end of row—40 (47, 50, 56) sts each side. Working both sides at the same time, dec 1 st at each neck edge every RS row 6 times, then every 4th row 8 times—26 (33, 36, 42) sts each side. Work even in St st until armhole measures 9 (10, 10, 11)"/23 (25.5, 25.5, 28)cm. Bind off. Center Front chart over front; with row 1 at first St st row, follow chart for Duplicate st (see page 111).

BACK

Work same as front, omitting neck shaping. Center Back chart over back; with row 1 at 10th St st row, follow chart for Duplicate st.

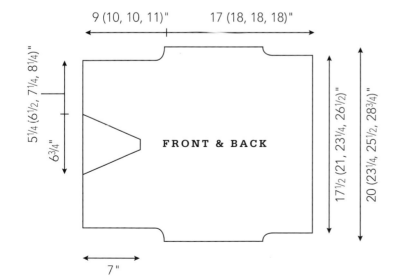

9 (10, 10, 11)"   17 (18, 18, 18)"

5¼ (6½, 7¼, 8¼)"

6¾"

FRONT & BACK

17½ (21, 23¼, 26½)"

20 (23¼, 25½, 28¾)"

7"

FINISHING

Sew shoulder seams. Sew side seams. Run a double-strand of A through each shoulder seam; gather shoulder width lightly and secure.

NECKBAND

With RS facing and circular needle, starting at base of neck shaping, pick up and k 48 sts along diagonal edge to shoulder seam, 36 sts across back neck, 48 sts along diagonal edge to base of neck shaping—132 sts.
Work in k2, p2 rib for 1¼"/3.25cm.
Next row Work to last 4 sts, turn.
Next row Work to last 4 sts, turn.
Next row Work to 4 sts before last turn, turn.
Rep last row 13 times more.
Last row Work to end of row.
Bind off in rib.

Overlap ends of neckband at center front and sew over center bound-off sts.

ARMBANDS

With RS facing and circular needle, starting at underarm seam, pick up and k 96 (108, 112, 128) sts evenly around armhole. Pm and join. Work in k2, p2 rib for 1"/2.5cm. Bind off in rib.

SIDE VENT CASING

With RS facing and circular needle, starting at lower edge, pick up and k 82 sts around to lower edge of other side. Work in k2, p2 rib, starting with p2 on first WS row, for 2"/5cm. Bind off knitwise. Fold band to WS and sew to pick up row to form a casing. Rep on other side.

CORD (make 2)

With dpns, cast on 4 sts. Work in I-cord (see page 111) for 30"/76cm. Bind off. Hook end of cord with safety pin and thread through casing. Tie a knot at each end of cord. ●

Play it again, Pan
This charming flute player was part of an Etruscan tomb fresco, circa 450 B.C.

84 STITCHES

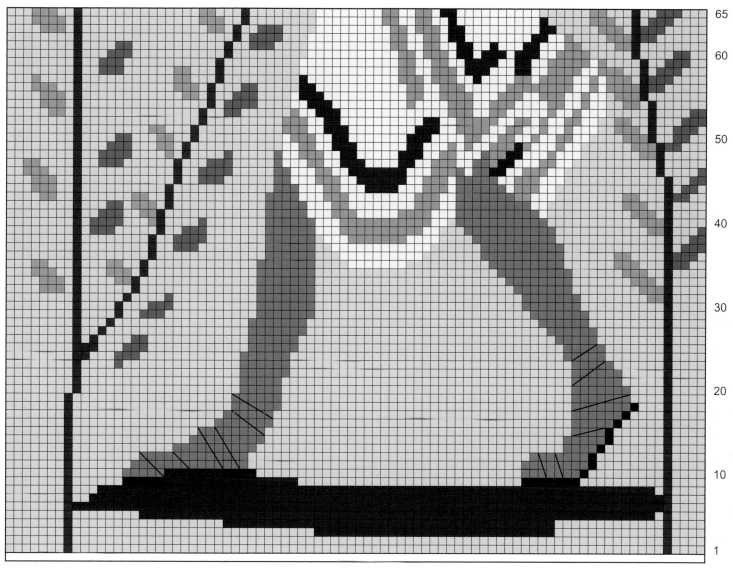

84 STITCHES

✤ *Color Key*

- ⬜ GOLD (A)
- 🟦 PINK (B)
- ⬛ BURGUNDY (C)
- 🟦 BLUE (D)
- ⬛ CHOCOLATE (E)

- 🟦 TAN (F)
- 🟦 GREEN (G)
- 🟦 OLIVE (H)
- ⬜ YELLOW (I)
- ⬛ BLACK (J)

✤ *Stitch Key*

＼ Straight Stitch with J

BACK LEFT SIDE

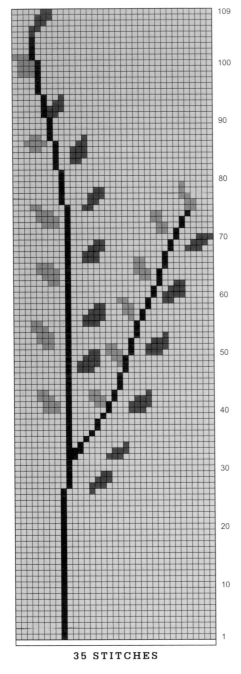

109
100
90
80
70
60
50
40
30
20
10
1

35 STITCHES

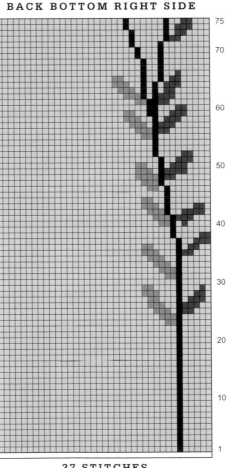

BACK BOTTOM RIGHT SIDE

75
70
60
50
40
30
20
10
1

37 STITCHES

BACK TOP RIGHT SIDE

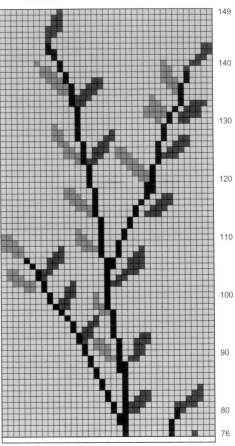

149
140
130
120
110
100
90
80
76

37 STITCHES

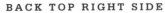

 Color Key

- ⬜ GOLD (A)
- 🟫 PINK (B)
- ⬛ BURGUNDY (C)
- 🟦 BLUE (D)
- ⬛ CHOCOLATE (E)
- 🟫 TAN (F)
- 🟩 GREEN (G)
- 🟫 OLIVE (H)
- ⬜ YELLOW (I)
- ⬛ BLACK (J)

Cypress Capelet

Cypress trees are found everywhere in Tuscany, and this lovely little cape captures their striking elegance.

SIZE
Finished length 24"/61cm
Lower edge width 52"/132cm

MATERIALS
❖ 5 50g skeins (each approx 153yds/140m) of Rowan/ Westminster Fibers, Inc. *Kid Classic,* 70% lambswool/26% kid mohair/4% nylon, in #853 spruce

❖ Size 7 (4.5mm) 40"/100cm circular needle, OR SIZE TO OBTAIN GAUGE

GAUGE
20 sts and 26 rows = 4"/10cm in St st
TAKE TIME TO CHECK GAUGE

SPECIAL ABBREVIATION
5-to-1 dec K2tog, k3tog, pass previous st over just made st.

CAPELET
Cast on 91 sts. Work in k1, p1 rib for 5"/12.5cm, end with a WS row.
Set-up row (RS) Work 7 sts in rib as est, *m1, p5, m1, k1; rep from * to last 12 sts, m1, p5, m1, work last 7 sts in rib as est—117 sts.
Row 1 (WS) Work 7 sts in rib, *k7, p1; rep from * to last 14 sts, k7, work 7 sts in rib.
Row 2 Work 7 sts in rib, *p7, k1; rep from * to last 14 sts, p7, work 7 sts in rib.
Rep last 2 rows 5 times more, then row 1 once more.
Inc row (RS) Work 7 sts in rib, *p7, m1, k1, m1; rep from * to last 14 sts, p7, work 7 sts in rib—141 sts.
Row 1 (WS) Work 7 sts in rib, *k7, p3; rep from * to last 14 sts, k7, work 7 sts in rib.
Row 2 Work 7 sts in rib, *p7, k3; rep from * to last 14 sts, p7, work 7 sts in rib.
Rep last 2 rows 3 times, then row 1 once more.
Inc row (RS) Work 7 sts in rib, *p7, m1, k3, m1; rep from * to last 14 sts, p7, work 7 sts in rib—165 sts.
Row 1 (WS) Work 7 sts in rib, *k7, p5; rep from * to last 14 sts, k7, work 7 sts in rib.
Row 2 Work 7 sts in rib, *p7, k5; rep from * to last 14 sts, p7, work 7 sts in rib.
Rep last 2 rows 2 times more, then row 1 once more.
Cont increasing 24 sts every 8th row 7 times more, working 2 more sts between m1 increases as est—333 sts.

Twist and turn
A typical Tuscan road winds around majestic cypress trees.

NOTE Last WS row will be as follows:
Work 7 sts in rib, *P7, K19; rep from* to last 14 sts, p7, work 7 sts in rib.

Continue as follows, with no further increasing:
Row 1 (RS) Work 7 sts in rib, p6, *k21, p5; rep from * to last 8 sts, p1, work 7 sts in rib.
Row 2 Work 7 sts in rib, k6, *p21, k5; rep from * to last 8 sts, k1, work 7 sts in rib.
Rows 3–6 Rep rows 1 and 2.
Row 7 Work 7 sts in rib, p5, *k23, p3; rep from * to last 9 sts, p2, work 7 sts in rib.
Row 8 Work 7 sts in rib, k5, *p23, k3; rep from * to last 9 sts, k2, work 7 sts in rib.
Rows 9–20 Rep rows 7 and 8.

EDGING
Row 1 Work 7 sts in rib, p5, *k6, 5-to-1 dec, k1, 5-to-1 dec, k6, p3; rep from * to last 9 sts, p2, work 7 sts in rib—237 sts.
Row 2 Work 7 sts in rib, k11, *m1, p3, m1, k15; rep from * to last 21 sts, m1, p3, m1, k11, work 7 sts in rib—261 sts.
Row 3 Work 7 sts in rib, p12, *k3, p17; rep from * to last 22 sts, k3, p12, work 7 sts in rib.
Row 4 Work 7 sts in rib, k12, *p3, k17; rep from * to last 22 sts, p3, k12, work 7 sts in rib.
Rows 5, 6 and 7 Rep rows 3 and 4, then row 3 once more.
Rows 8, 9 and 10 Work 7 sts in rib, k to last 7 sts, work 7 sts in rib.
Bind off loosely in patts as est.●

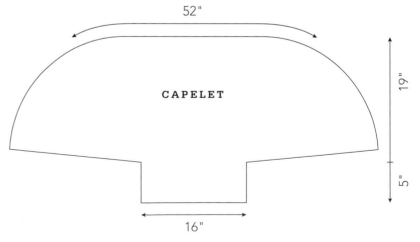

52"

CAPELET

19"

5"

16"

Carrara Marble Cardigan

The grays, pinks and greens of the legendary Carrara marble come to life in this colorful striped sweater.

SIZES
S (M/L, XL)
Finished bust 35 (47, 58)"/87.5 (117.5, 147.5)cm
Finished length 19½ (21½, 23½)"/49.5 (54.5, 59.5)cm

MATERIALS
❖ 6 (8, 10) 100g hanks (each approx 75yds/67m) of Alchemy Yarns of Transformation *Lux*, 30% silk/70% wool, in #9C diamonda (A)

❖ 5 (7, 9) hanks in #9M pewter (B)

❖ 2 (3, 3) hanks in #80A hush (C)

❖ 1 (2, 3) hanks in #23E good earth (D)

❖ Size 10½ (6.5mm) 40"/100cm circular needle, OR SIZE TO OBTAIN GAUGE

❖ Tapestry needle

GAUGE
14 sts and 18 rows = 4" (10cm) in pattern st
TAKE TIME TO CHECK GAUGE

MEASUREMENTS
Back
Width 17½ (23½, 29)"/44.5 (60, 73.5)cm
Length to underarm 12 (12½, 13)"/30.5 (31.75, 33)cm
Raglan depth 7½ (9, 10½)"/19 (22.75, 26.5)cm
Back neck 5¾ (6¾, 8)"/14.5 (17, 20.25)cm

Front
Width 9 (12, 14¾)"/23 (30.5, 37.5)cm
Front neck 3 (3¾, 4¼)"/5 (9.5, 10.75)cm

Sleeve
Cuff 9 (12, 12)"/22.75 (30.5, 30.5)cm
Length to underarm 17½ (18, 18½)"/44.5 (45.75, 47)cm
Upper arm width 16 (18¾, 22¼)"/40.5 (47.5, 56.5)cm
Side neck 4 (2¼, 1)"/10 (5.5, 2.5)cm

Front band width 4¼"/10.75cm

PATTERN ST (multiple of 10 sts + 2)
Row 1 (RS) Knit.
Row 2 Purl.
Row 3 K2, *p8, k2; rep from * to end.
Row 4 P2, *k8, p2; rep from * to end.
Row 5 K2, *p2, k4, p2, k2; rep from * to end.
Row 6 P2, *k2, p4, k2, p2; rep from * to end.
Rows 7–10 Rep rows 5 and 6.
Rows 11 and 12 Rep rows 3 and 4.
Rep rows 1–12 for pattern unless otherwise stated.

BODY STRIPE PATTERN
Work rows 1–12 with B, *rows 1–6 with C, rows 1–6 with D, rows 1–12 with A, rows 1–10 with B, rows 1–10 with A, rows 1–10 with B; rep from *.

SLEEVE STRIPE PATTERN
*Work rows 1–10 with A, rows 1–10 with C, rows 1–10 with D, rows 1–10 with B; rep from *.

BACK
With A and larger needle, cast on 62 (82, 102) sts. Work rows 2–10 of patt, then rep rows 5 and 6 until piece measures 4 (4½, 5)"/10 (11.5, 12.75)cm from beg. Work rows 11 and 12.
Work in Body stripe patt until piece measures 12 (12½, 13)"/30.5 (31.75, 33)cm from beg, end with a WS row.

RAGLAN SHAPING
Cont in Body stripe patt, bind off 4 (9, 13) sts at beg of next 2 rows.
Dec row (RS) Ssk, work in patt as est to last 2 sts, k2tog.
Rep dec row every RS row until 20 (24, 28) sts rem. Bind off.

LEFT FRONT

With A and larger needle, cast on 32 (42, 52) sts. Work same as Back until piece measures 12 (12 ½, 13)"/30.5, 31.75, 33)cm from beg, end with a WS row. **Note** Stripe pattern should match back.

RAGLAN SHAPING

Cont in Body stripe patt, bind off 4 (9, 13) sts at beg of next row. Work 1 WS row.
Dec row (RS) Ssk, work in patt to end of row.
Rep dec row every RS row until 11 (13, 15) sts rem. Bind off.

RIGHT FRONT

With A and larger needle, cast on 32 (42, 52) sts. Work same as Back until piece measures 12 (12½, 13)"/30.5, 31.75, 33)cm from beg, end with a RS row. Note Stripe pattern should match back.

RAGLAN SHAPING

Cont in Body stripe patt, bind off 4 (9, 13) sts at beg of next row.
Dec row (RS) Work in patt to last 2 sts, k2tog.
Rep dec row every RS row until 11 (13, 15) sts rem. Bind off.

SLEEVES

With B, cast on 32 (42, 42) sts. Work in Sleeve stripe pat, beg with row 2 and inc 1 st each side starting with first row of C, then every 6th (6th, 4th) row 11(11, 17) times more, incorporating new sts into patt—56 (66, 78) sts. Work even in patt as est until sleeve measures 17½ (18, 18½)"/44.5 (45.75, 47)cm or desired length from beg, end with a WS row.

RAGLAN SHAPING

Bind off 4 (9, 13) sts at beg of next 2 rows.
Dec row (RS) Ssk, work in patt as est to last 2 sts, k2tog.
Rep dec row every RS row until 14 (8, 4) sts rem. Place sts on holder.

COLLAR AND FRONT BANDS

With A, cast on 232 (242, 262) sts. Work rows 1–6 of patt st; change to B and work rows 1–6; change to A and work rows 1–6. K1 RS row. Bind off purlwise on WS.

FINISHING

Sew raglan seams. Sew side and sleeve seams. Sew bound-off edge of collar and front bands to fronts and neck opening, making a 1"/2.5cm inverted pleat at each neck edge. Use a shawl pin to close. ●

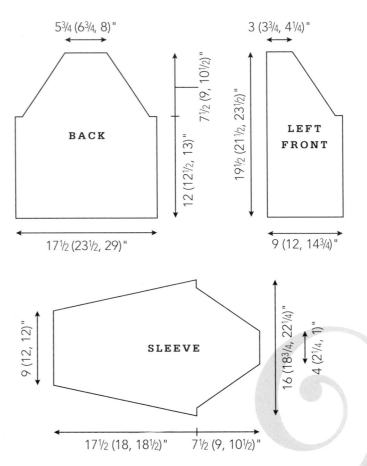

5¾ (6¾, 8)"

3 (3¾, 4¼)"

BACK

7½ (9, 10½)"

12 (12½, 13)"

19½ (21½, 23½)"

LEFT FRONT

17½ (23½, 29)"

9 (12, 14¾)"

9 (12, 12)"

SLEEVE

16 (18¾, 22¼)"

4 (2¼, 1)"

17½ (18, 18½)"   7½ (9, 10½)"

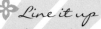

Line it up

Siena's Duomo is one of a number of Italian cathedrals striped with varying shades of Carrara marble.

Chianti is a place to relax, take long walks or short drives and sip a glass of *vino*.

Chianti

Chianti

Getting just a little tired of art masterpieces, designer boutiques and big-town traffic? Head for Chianti. This laid-back, bucolic area of Tuscany is known for its famous wine, Chianti Classico. As you travel the Via Chiantigiana, known as the *Strada del Vino* (Wine Road) and connecting Florence and Siena, you'll pass ancient castles, stone farmhouses, delightful villages, olive groves and miles and miles of vineyards. Spending a few days in this part of Tuscany will lower your blood pressure and put you in touch with the leisurely Italian lifestyle.

GREVE IN CHIANTI

Greve is a great base for visiting all of Chianti. It's centered around the triangular Piazza Giacomo Matteotti, which is dominated by a statue of Giovanni da Verrazzano (born nearby), discoverer of New York Harbor. The piazza is filled with cafés, restaurants, and food and gift shops. It hosts a wonderful market on Saturday, and there's even a well-stocked supermarket, the Coop, just a couple of blocks away. Greve is also the scene of a carousing wine fair in September.

ACCOMMODATIONS

Have you ever wanted to stay in a castle? I have…and I did! **Castello Vicchiomaggio** (Via Vicchiomaggio 4; vicchiomaggio.it) just north of Greve is my favorite place in the world to stay (Leonardo was a guest here, too). It is a beautiful sixteenth-century Renaissance castle and winery that rents spectacular rooms and apartments at fairly reasonable rates. Our duplex apartment, which overlooked a beautiful courtyard, was enormous (larger than our apartment in New York), had a 20-foot ceiling and was filled with antique furniture. The Castello has a pool, a breathtaking view of vineyards in the Greve valley below, and best of all, a lovely garden filled with trees, flowers and benches. I felt like a princess knitting in the garden. This is a popular place, so make reservations well in advance of your trip.

DINING

At **Da Verrazzano** (Piazza Giacomo Matteotti 28; ristoranteverrazzano.it), you can dine on the terrace overlooking the piazza. *Crostini,* mixed salami, pasta with mushrooms, rabbit, and the house Chianti are especially good. Just up the hill from Greve is the castle and walled village of Castello di Montefioralle, one of the oldest in Tuscany. The ancient, narrow streets are wonderful to stroll through, and as you walk around the circular inner road you will come upon the **Taverna del Guerrino** (greve-in-chianti.com/guerrino.htm). It has fantastic views inside and out. Try the roasted meats (especially the ribs) and the coconut ice cream for dessert. **La Cantinetta di Rignana** (lacantinettadirignana.it), near Greve in Rignana, is a family-run, rustic farmhouse restaurant. The dining room is beautiful, but the view from the outdoor terrace is sensational. Dine on mixed antipasti, *taglierini* with butter and sage, thick *ribollita,* wood-grilled meats and game, apple tart and *panna cotta,* all served by helpful and cheerful people. It's well worth the 25-minute drive from Greve.

SIGHTSEEING

The best sightseeing in Chianti is the villages themselves. The scenery as you drive the roads and visit the vineyards and wineries is stunning, but make sure you visit **Vignamaggio**, a beautiful Renaissance villa that you can tour along with its

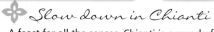
Slow down in Chianti

A feast for all the senses, Chianti is a wonderful place to sightsee, eat, drink wine, or just sit back and knit.

A Visit to the Chianti Cashmere Farm

Imagine being in the beautiful Tuscan countryside looking at more cashmere than you've ever seen. And what's more, that cashmere is looking back at you!

The **Chianti Cashmere Farm & Company** (chianticashmere.com) just outside of Radda in Chianti is the pride and the passion of New Yorker Nora Kravis. In 1972, the fabric designer came to Tuscany with a fine-arts degree, an unbounded affection for animals and an adventurous spirit. She found a ramshackle farmhouse on seven acres with spectacular Tuscan views and set about restoring the farm into a lovely home and rental villa. She also attended the University of Pisa to study veterinary medicine. Her dream was to start a cashmere goat farm, but all the experts told her that was impossible to do in the warm Tuscan environment. Impossible is not a word that Nora recognizes, so in 1988 she bought her first two cashmere goats. After years of hard work, selective breeding, creative animal husbandry, genetic improvement techniques and a lot of love, she now owns the only herd of cashmere goats (over 200) in Italy and produces some of the finest cashmere in the world. So much for the "experts."

On the day we visited, Nora gave us an up-close-and-personal tour. She showed us how the goats are combed to obtain their wool, the fine underfibers are separated from the rougher outer fibers, and the fine fibers are hand-spun into the soft, warm, light yarn knitters dream about.

When you visit her, you'll love her charming shop, with its selection of handmade cashmere scarves, shawls, blankets, throws and sweaters in lovely natural colors and newly developed dyed colors. She also produces an amazing line of soaps and skincare products made from goat's milk.

And, if you want to get away from it all, Nora rents a charming three-bedroom house with private garden, terrace and pool overlooking the beautiful Volpaia Valley. (But no goats are permitted in the rooms, no matter how chummy you get with them.)

Nora and I have become friends over the years, and we try to get together whenever she makes her infrequent trips back to New York. I've knit a piece in this book with her gorgeous cashmere yarn (see page 78).

1

2

3

DAY TRIP

Castellina in Chianti

Castellina is a charming hilltop village with an impressive fortress called the **Rocca Communale** and lots of restaurants, accommodations and shopping. Take a walk down the fifteenth-century underground vaulted street **Via delle Volte,** and you'll come upon a little shop carrying all kinds of handbags at great prices. On the main street, we visited the **Palazzo Squarcialupi** (Via Ferrucio 22). It has lovely rooms and an exquisite, ornate spa. ●

✤ *Down on the farm*
1 Cashmere sweaters in their natural state. **2** Nora, me and a couple of kids. **3** Some of Nora's lovely cashmere scarves.

magnificent gardens. Actor-director Kenneth Branagh shot his film *Much Ado About Nothing* here, and Lisa Gherardini, aka Mona Lisa, was reportedly born here.

SHOPPING

You can spend an interesting couple of hours in the shops around the piazza, but be sure to stop in at **Antica Macelleria Falorni** (Piazza Giacomo Matteotti 71; falorni.it), a shop that makes its own hams, sausages, salamis and other pork products, along with artisanal cheeses and condiments. The aromas will have you drooling! **Dinterni e Dintorni** (Via Roma 35), located just off the square, sells unusual antiques.

PANZANO IN CHIANTI

This tiny town down the road from Greve is worth the stop to wander the narrow cobblestone streets, enjoy the countryside views and visit the most famous butcher in Tuscany (see page 106).

ACCOMMODATIONS

Villa Rosa de Boscorotondo (Via San Leolino 59; resortvillarosa.it), just outside Panzano off Via Chiantigiana (SS 222), is a large pink villa that exudes rustic elegance. Run by the charming Giancarlo and Sabina Avuri and their son Neri, this wonder has rooms with curtained wrought-iron beds, tasteful antique furnishings and private bathrooms at reasonable rates. There is a pool out back, a lovely garden patio where breakfast is served and free parking. (And just up the hill are the vineyards and shop of the Il Molino di Grace Winery, which is owned by an American.) Ask for one of the front rooms that have private terraces overlooking the countryside. We dined on our terrace one evening, and it was an amazing experience.

DINING

On our last trip to Chianti, we dined at **Trattoria Oltre il Giardino** (Piazza Bucciarelli 42; ristoranteoltreilgiardino.it) twice. Although the interior, with its fireplace, is cozy and lovely, the terrace, with its tables under a hanging wisteria tree and its wonderful view of the valley, is *the* place for dinner. Dine on plates of Tuscan salami, polenta with mushroom sauce, beef in pepper sauce, sausage and ribs, and a ruby-red Vigna Piccola Chianti from Panzano.

SIGHTSEEING

Walk the narrow streets in the old section of town and you'll come upon the church of **Santa Maria Assunta**, which has one of the most striking facades I have ever seen.

RADDA IN CHIANTI

Radda is a high-walled, beautifully preserved town that is an important wine center. Near Radda is the incredible Chianti Cashmere Farm (see opposite).

ACCOMODATIONS

La Locanda (lalocanda.it) is a charming hotel that has seven lovely country-style rooms. The views over the Radda Valley and the town of Volpaia are sensational, and there's even a pool.

DINING

Stop for lunch at **La Perla del Palazzo** (Via Roma 33) for panoramic views and delicious Tuscan cuisine. The salads are super.

SIGHTSEEING

Walking down the ancient **Via Roma,** you pass a lion's-head fountain and come to the **Palazzo del Podestà** (town hall), which is covered with coats of arms. Wander down some of the picturesque back streets and browse the interesting shops.

Chianti Rooster Pillow

A black rooster is the symbol of the Chianti Classico Wine Producers' Association and is found on every bottle of that luscious liquid. This felted pillow is an homage to the lovely red wine.

SIZE
Approx 20"W x 22"L/51 x 56cm, before felting

Approx 16½" x 17½"/42 x 44.5cm, after felting

MATERIALS
❖ 3 50g hanks (each approx 109yds/99m) of Dale of Norway *Heilo*, 100% wool, each in #90 black (A) and #4018 red (B)

❖ Size 9 (5.5mm) needles OR SIZE TO OBTAIN GAUGE

❖ Size 5 (3.75mm) double-pointed needles

❖ One 12"/30.5cm zipper (optional)

❖ One 16"/40.5cm square pillow form or one bag of polyester fiberfill

GAUGE
Approx 15 sts and 24 rows = 4"/10cm in St st using larger needles, before felting
TAKE TIME TO CHECK GAUGE

NOTE
Pillow back wraps around to sides of front.

FRONT
With B, cast on 65 sts. Work 126 rows of chart in St st. Bind off.

BACK
With A, cast on 105 sts. Work stripes in St st as follows: 9 rows A, [12 rows B, 12 rows A] 4 times, 12 rows B, 9 rows A. Bind off.

COCKSCOMB FRINGE
With A and dpns, cast on 3 sts. Work in I-cord (see page 111) for 4 yds/3.5m.
Slip sts onto larger needle and divide cord into 7 sections as folls: first section 18"/45.5cm, rem 6 sections 21"/53.5cm each.
Pick-up row With first section, make 3 loops approx 3½"/9cm, 3"/7.5cm and 2½"/6.5cm high. Pick up and k2 sts in the 2 loop bottoms. *With the next section, pick up and k8 sts across 3"/7.5cm of cord, make 3 loops and pick up and k4 sts as for first section; rep from *, picking up and knitting 9 sts at beg of next and every other section—85 sts.
K 2 rows. Bind off.

FINISHING
Sew side seams. Sew top seam, then sew bottom seam, leaving 13½"/33.5cm open at center. Sew fringe to top edge of pillow.

Felt pillow (see page 26). Let dry completely. Sew in zipper and insert pillow form. Alternatively, stuff with fiberfill and sew opening closed. ●

65 STITCHES

In Tuscany, the rooster
represents good fortune.
Knitting one will bring
you luck.

Cashmere Necklette

I knit the soft circles for this luxurious piece with Sustainable Cashmere® from Chianti Cashmere (see page 72). You can order it online or use the yarn listed below.

SIZES
Approx 6¼"W x 37½"L/16 x 95.5cm

MATERIALS
❖ 1 55g hank (each approx 400yds/360m) of Jade Sapphire Exotic Fibres *Mongolian Cashmere 2-ply* in #50 driftwood (A)

❖ 1 hank #74 black walnut (B)

❖ Size 3 (3.25mm) double-pointed needles (set of 5)
OR SIZE TO OBTAIN GAUGE

❖ Size D (3.25mm) crochet hook

❖ Stitch marker

❖ Tapestry needle

❖ 72 size 8/0 glass beads (12 for each medallion)

❖ Embroidery needle (should fit through beads)

GAUGE
36 sts and 40 rows = 4"/10cm in St st
TAKE TIME TO CHECK GAUGE
Finished medallion measures 6¼"/16cm in diameter

STAR MEDALLION (make 6)
With A, cast on 8 sts. Divide evenly over 4 needles, pm and join.
Rnd 1 *K1 tbl; rep from * to end.
Rnd 2 *Yo, k1; rep from * to end—16 sts.
Rnd 3 and all odd-numbered rnds Knit.
Rnd 4 *Yo, k2; rep from * to end—24 sts.
Rnd 6 *Yo, k3; rep from * to end—32 sts.
Rnd 8 *Yo, k4; rep from * to end—40 sts.
Rnd 10 *Yo, k5; rep from * to end—48 sts.
Rnd 12 *Yo, k6; rep from * to end—56 sts.
Rnd 14 *Yo, k7; rep from * to end—64 sts.
Rnd 16 *Yo, k8; rep from * to end—72 sts.
Rnd 18 *Yo, k1, yo, ssk, k6; rep from * to end—80 sts.
Rnd 20 *Yo, k1, [yo, ssk] twice, k5; rep from * to end—88 sts.
Rnd 22 *Yo, k1, [yo, ssk] 3 times, k4; rep from * to end—96 sts.
Rnd 24 *Yo, k1, [yo, ssk] 4 times, k3; rep from * to end—104 sts.
Rnd 26 *Yo, k1, [yo, ssk] 5 times, k2; rep from * to end—112 sts.
Rnd 28 *Yo, k1, [yo, ssk] 6 times, k1; rep from * to end—120 sts.
Rnd 30 *Yo, k1, [yo, ssk] 7 times; rep from * to end—128 sts.
Rnd 31 Bind off.
With B, work 1 row of single crochet around medallion.

FINISHING
Sew 12 beads to center of each medallion. Sew medallions end to end, sewing 3"/7.5cm between 2 star points. ●

Pamper yourself!
You'll be chic *and* cozy in this incredibly soft and light neck warmer.

Vineyard Bag

Vineyards dominate the Chianti countryside. The colors and shape of these world famous Tuscan grapes were the inspiration for this heirloom clutch bag.

SIZE
Approx 7"H x 7"W/ 17.75 x 17.75cm

MATERIALS
❖ 1 2oz hank (each approx 210 yds/189m) of Fiesta Yarns *La Luz Multi*, 100% spun silk, in clematis

❖ One pair size 6 (4mm) needles OR SIZE TO OBTAIN GAUGE

❖ Tapestry needle

❖ 15" x 8"/30.5 x 20.5cm fabric for lining

❖ Vintage-style 4"/10cm bag frame (Sunbelt Fastener Co. #SFPF-C42AB in gold or #SFPF-C42AN in silver, or from Lacis—#LS39)

GAUGE
22 sts and 24 rows to 4"/10cm in Seed st
TAKE TIME TO CHECK GAUGE

SEED ST
Row 1 K1, *p1, k1; rep from * to end.
Rep row 1 for patt.

BAG
Starting at top edge, cast on 15 sts.
Row 1 (WS) *Kfb; rep from * to last st, k1—29 sts.
Work in Seed st, inc 1 st each edge every RS row 4 times—37 sts, incorporating new sts into patt.
Cont even in Seed st until piece measures 10"/25.5cm from beg.
Work in Seed st, dec 1 st each edge every RS row 4 times—29 sts.
Last row K2tog, *k2tog, pass first st over 2nd st; rep from * to last st, slip last st and pass first st over.
Fasten off.

GRAPES (make 17)
Make a slip knot and place on needle.
Row 1 (RS) K in front, back, front, back, front of st—5 sts.
Row 2 Purl.
Row 3 Knit.
Row 4 Purl.
Row 5 K2tog, k1, k2tog—3 sts.
Row 6 Sl 1, p2tog, psso—1 st.
Fasten off, leaving 3"/4cm tails.

STEM
Using green section of yarn, cast on 9 sts, bind off 9 sts.

EDGING
Cast on 126 sts.
Row 1 (WS) *K1, bind off next 7 sts; rep from * to end.
Row 2 K1, *cast on 4 sts, k2; rep from *, end last rep k1—84 sts.
Row 3 Knit.
Bind off.

FINISHING
Position grapes and stem on front of bag (use photo for guide). Thread cast-on and bound-off tails through to WS to tie or sew in place. Sew side seams. Make lining to fit. Attach bag frame following instructions. (Note: If using this frame, unscrew the 3 small screws, insert lining and replace screws.) Sew edging evenly around side and bottom edges of bag. ●

❦ *Lady of the vines*
As the song goes, "From the vine came the grape...from the grape came the wine."

The hills are alive...
Each Tuscan hill town has its own personality
and breathtaking views.

Montepulciano,
Montalcino and
Cortona

MONTEPULCIANO is one of the largest and highest walled hill towns in Tuscany. Walking through its medieval streets, which are filled with splendid Renaissance palaces and churches, is a real treat. All the walking might just make you thirsty, but you're in luck, because this town is home to Vino Nobile di Montepulciano, the noble wine that many consider to be "the king of all wines," and there are *enoteche* (wine bars; sing.: *enoteca*) and *cantine* (wine cellars; sing. *cantina*) everywhere. You can also sample these wines at the Consorzio del Vino Nobile di Montepulciano showroom and tasting center (Piazza Grande 7; consorziovinonobile.it). Montepulciano—drink it in!

ACCOMODATIONS

Near the entrance to the town is the largest hotel within the town walls, **Albergo Il Marzocco** (Piazza Savonarol 18; cretedisiena.com/albergoilmarzocco). It has parking nearby, and room #24 has a balcony with a great view of the countryside.

DINING

One of the best lunches we had in Tuscany was on Montepulciano's main street at the **Antico Caffè Poliziano** (Via Voltaia nel Corso 27; montepulciano .com/caffepoliziano), a beautiful Art Nouveau restaurant that dates back to 1868. We were just about to sit down when we spotted a small table outside on a tiny terrace and asked to be seated there. It was a great decision. The weather was perfect, the sky was a vivid blue with fluffy white clouds drifting by and the view over the Val di Chiana (Chiana Valley) looked like a painting. The food matched the view: plates of local salami, pâtés and sausages, a salad right out of the garden, a dessert of fresh peaches and an assortment of extraordinary cheeses all topped off with a bottle of Vino Nobile di Montepulciano. I didn't want to leave, and I occasionally dream about that lunch—that is, when I'm not dreaming about my next knitting project. There is also an art gallery in the basement of the restaurant, and they have jazz concerts there during the month of July.

SIGHTSEEING

The main square, **Piazza Grande,** has three impressive palazzi (palaces)—**Comunale, Tarugi,** and **Contucci**—and the **Duomo,** all worthy of a visit. On a hillside just below the town walls sits the **Madonna di San Biagio,** a beautiful church considered to be a perfect example of Renaissance architecture. Get out your camera!

MONTALCINO is a beautiful, medieval walled town situated on a high hill overlooking vineyards that produce one of Tuscany's finest wines, Brunello di Montalcino (and its baby brother Rosso di Montalcino). Driving to Montalcino from any direction will give you photo-ops of the magnificent Tuscan countryside.

ACCOMMODATIONS

The place to stay is the ultra-charming thirteenth-century residence **Palazzina Cesira** (Via Soccorso Saloni 2; montalcinoitaly.com), which is run by the warm and charming Lucilla and Roberto. Roberto lived in the United States for many years, speaks perfect English and is a font of information for what to do and see in and around Montalcino.

Pienza

A day trip (actually a half-day trip) to the serene, small town of Pienza is very rewarding. Walking through the tiny town is a tranquil experience as you explore the **Piazza Pio II** with its Duomo and impressive *cisterna* (well). The main street, **Corso Rossellino,** goes from one end of town to the other and can be walked in two minutes, unless you stop at the ceramic and food shops along the way. Franco Zeffirelli filmed his *Romeo and Juliet* here rather than in Verona, and many scenes from *The English Patient* were also shot here. A pleasant lunch can be had at the **Trattoria Latte di Luna** (Via San Carlo 4), which serves dishes like *zuppa di pane* (a local version of *ribollita)* and *maialino arrosto* (roast suckling pig) along with homemade desserts. Pienza is a quiet treat.

montepulciano

❧ *The good life, Tuscan-style*

Take time out for a "light" lunch before resuming your sightseeing and yarn hunting. A glass or two of Vino Nobile di Montepulciano will top it off nicely.

The lovely Lucilla will cook you a great breakfast and make you feel that you are visiting the home of good friends. Parking is available close by, just outside the walls.

DINING
There are some wonderful restaurants in and around Montalcino. A great place to start is lunch at the **Enoteca Osteria Osticcio** (Via Matteotti 23), a combination wine store and restaurant where you can sample a number of Brunellos along with meats, cheese plates and crusty Tuscan bread, all while enjoying a spectacular view out the panoramic windows.

We had a wonderful dinner at the beautifully decorated **Re di Macchia Ristorante** (Via Saloni 21)—*pici con ragù di cinghiale,* prosciutto stuffed with ricotta, large ravioli in a truffle sauce and a delicious Rosso di Montalcino.

SIGHTSEEING
Montalcino is a small town easily seen by just walking around enjoying the shops and eating establishments, lovely medieval buildings and panoramic views of the surrounding valleys and vineyards. The main attraction is the impressive fourteenth-century **Fortezza** (fortress), now home to the fabulous Sagra del Tordo festival (see 89). Walk the ramparts on the walls for incredible views (make sure you've got lots of film or digital memory cards, because it's hard to stop taking pictures throughout Tuscany). Inside the Fortezza is an *enoteca* where bottles of Brunello are sold. You can also purchase glasses of these delicious wines along with prosciutto, salami and cheese.

One day we drove up to a high, small vineyard and winery outside Montalcino called **Tenuta Di Sesta** and purchased a bottle of their 1997 Brunello (a magnificent vintage). To this day, it is the best wine I have ever had. From there we went on to the beautiful **Abbey of Sant'Antimo,** set in a lush valley surrounded by pigeons and white cows. We were privileged to hear the Augustinian monks who tend the church singing hauntingly beautiful Gregorian chants. The whole experience was surreal.

We then drove to the **Castello Banfi Estate** (castellobanfi.com), one of the largest wineries in Italy, with 7,100 acres. It is owned by the Mariani family of Long Island, New York, and a tour of the castle, winery and cellars makes for a great afternoon. We had a late lunch in their taverna. All they had left was *ribollita* and spaghetti, but both were sensational. We topped off the meal with pastries and a wonderful dessert wine from Sicily.

Once when we were on a leisurely drive near Montalcino, a truck was following us, its horn honking in annoyance at our slow speed. Finally the driver pulled in front of us, stopped and got out, shouting and gesturing as he advanced toward us. We simply said, "Mea culpa" (I'm sorry), and it stopped him in his tracks. He ceased shouting, threw up his arms and got back in his truck, looking crestfallen, then drove away. He was terribly disappointed that we didn't argue back!

CORTONA, originally established by the Etruscans, is a charming walled town that is easy to explore. Its popularity has exploded since it was featured in the popular book and movie *Under the Tuscan Sun,* but even with all the tourists, it's still a wonderful place to visit. Cortona, like most Tuscan hill towns, is wonderful to just walk around day or night. There are hilly streets and stairs to contend with (the Via Nazionale is the only flat street and is called *Ruga Piana—* "level street"—by locals), but if you wear those incredibly comfortable shoes you

brought and pace yourself, you should have no problem.

Once, when we were in Cortona, a film crew showed up to shoot some scenes for *Under the Tuscan Sun.* They filled the main piazza, Piazza della Repubblica, with fake snow, and we watched them film a couple of scenes that night. The next day we ran into an actual wedding with the bride and groom coming down the town hall stairs, which were still covered in fake snow. But that's the wonderful thing about Tuscany—you never know what fun surprises you'll run into.

ACCOMODATIONS

The **Hotel San Michele** (Via Guelfa 15; hotelsanmichele.net) is a converted eleventh-century palace just off the Piazza della Repubblica. It has charming, moderately sized rooms with plaster walls and vaulted, wood-beamed ceilings. Some of the rooms have beautiful views. The hotel serves a filling breakfast with a delicious, thick hot chocolate, and there is indoor parking a couple of blocks away.

DINING

My very favorite restaurant in Cortona is the rustic **Trattoria la Grotta** (Piazza Baldelli 3). It has a friendly staff and wonderful dishes like tagliatelle with truffle oil, grilled sausages and spinach and *pappardelle* with *cinghiale* that reminds me of a sauce my grandmother made. At dessert, try the delectable *biscotti* with a glass of *vin santo.* Another nice restaurant is the **Ristorante La Loggetta** (Piazza di Pescherio 3). You can dine on the terrace in good weather and look down on the Piazza della Repubblica as you put away *bistecca alla fiorentina,* roast potatoes and a nice red house wine. Saturday

morning is market day, with lots of wonderful fresh food and crafts. I had an incredible pork sandwich with crackling skin on it that I can almost taste today. You will eat a lot in Tuscany, but the good news is you'll walk it off.

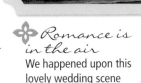

Romance is in the air
We happened upon this lovely wedding scene during our stay in Cortona.

SIGHTSEEING

The main square in town is the **Piazza della Repubblica.** There you'll find the handsome thirteenth-century **Palazzo Communale** (town hall). On the adjoining Piazza Signorelli sits the **Palazzo Pretorio** (or Palazzo Casali), which houses the **Museo dell'Accademia Etrusca** (Etruscan Museum). The museum has a treasure of artifacts and features an outstanding Etruscan chandelier in its great central hall. I love this museum, and it inspired one of my knitted designs (see page 98). The eleventh-century **Duomo** at the Piazza del Duomo is impressive; in the same square is the **Museo Diocesano,** with several masterpieces by Fra Angelico, Lorenzetti and Signorelli. A remarkable Renaissance church, **Santa Maria delle Grazie,** can be reached by a fifteen-minute uphill walk, or you can drive up. The church and the view of the surrounding countryside are worth it.

SHOPPING

The main street and primary shopping street is the **Via Nazionale.** It has many touristy and non-touristy shops like **Il Cocciano,** which carries a large selection of earthenware in colors typical of the countryside around Cortona—the yellow of the cornfields, the brown and green of the forests. There is also a shop on the street that carries yarn and needles.●

EXPLORING
Sagra del Tordo

There are many wonderful festivals throughout Tuscany, but my favorite is the medieval Sagra del Tordo (Thrush Festival), which is held on the last weekend of October in Montalcino. It is almost worth planning your Tuscany trip around it so you can be there for the festivities.

The festival dates back to an old hunting tradition celebrating the migration of the thrushes from the north each fall. For two days, Montalcino goes all out with pageantry, parades, costumes, music, dancing, archery contests and nonstop eating and drinking (Brunello, of course).

The festival opens with boys and girls in colorful costumes singing and dancing in the main square. Then a procession of locals in medieval costume marches to trumpets and drums through the streets up to the Fortezza. Throngs of locals and tourists get caught up in the spirit of the festival. The procession winds up at an archery field where the "Lady of the Fortress" and her court await.

A highlight of the festivities is an intense archery competition between the four *quartieri* (quarters) of Montalcino: Borghetto, Pianello, Ruga and Travaglio (each with its own colors and banners). The winning team gets a silver arrow and celebrates with an all-night banquet.

In the courtyard of the Fortezza, vendors set up booths selling tagliatelle with wild boar sauce, *pici* with meat sauce, grilled meats and sausages, polenta, pastries, and, of course, Brunello di Montalcino. Traditionally, hundreds of thrush were cooked on spits over open fires, but in recent years the thrush population has declined, so now they roast squab. This tiny bird is delicious!

The festivities go on into the evening with eating, drinking and music. It is a once-in-a-lifetime experience. At the festival I was stopped in my tracks. One of the vendors looked exactly like my grandfather Aneilio DeFazio, who was from Avellino near Naples. We managed to take a picture of him, and when I showed it to my uncles back home, they swore it was their father. Another Tuscan surprise! ●

DAY TRIP
Arezzo

An easy day trip from Cortona to the town of Arezzo will be a treat you'll always remember. Arezzo has beautiful churches and two fine piazzas—**Grande** and **della Repubblica,** but the main attraction is the thirteenth-century **Basilica of San Francesco** with Piero della Francesca's stunning frescoes. The frescoes have been beautifully restored and are truly awe-inspiring.

And while you're there, how about an awe-inspiring lunch at the **Ristorante Buca di San Francesco** (Via San Francesco 1)? Its décor is as wonderful as its food (especially the *pappardelle* with duck and rabbit sauce). ●

Abbondanza Wrap

I created the felted balls that adorn this colorful wrap with hazelnuts. Hazelnuts abound in Tuscany and are used to make the legendary liqueur Frangelico.

SIZE
Approx 20½"W x 68"L/52 x 172.75cm, before felting
Approx 11"W x 36"L/28 x 91.5cm, after felting

MATERIALS
❖ 3 100g hanks (each approx 191yds/175m) of Colinette/Unique Kolours, Ltd. *Mohair*, 78% mohair/ 13% wool/9% nylon, in #55 toscana

❖ Size 10 (6mm) needles
OR SIZE TO OBTAIN GAUGE

❖ Approx 250 hazelnuts and small rubber bands

❖ 2yds/1.75m 1¾"/4.5cm-wide ribbon

❖ Sewing needle and matching thread

GAUGE
16 sts and 22 rows = 4"/10cm in St st, before felting
TAKE TIME TO CHECK GAUGE

Cast on 82 sts. Work in St st until piece measures 68"/172.75cm from beg. Bind off.

Place nuts randomly onto WS of piece, securing with rubber bands on the RS. Felt piece (see page 26). Let dry completely. Remove rubber bands and nuts.

Cut ribbon in half. Sew one end of each piece to upper corners of wrap

NOTE Mohair may tangle into rubber bands. Gently cut rubber bands out with small, sharp scissors.●

BEFORE FELTING

montepulciano

Bella Bride's Dress

This crocheted dress was inspired by my Italian grandmother's handmade doilies. Wear it and you can be a contessa in Cortona or a bride in Brooklyn.

SIZES

Bust 34"/86.5cm
Waist 30"/76cm
Hip 38"/96.5cm
Front length 53"/134.5cm
Back length 63"/160cm

MATERIALS

❖ 18 50g hanks (each approx 135 yds/121m) of Tilli Tomas *Elsie,* 34% silk/33% merino wool/33% milk protein, in white

❖ Size D (3.25mm) crochet hook, OR SIZE TO OBTAIN GAUGE

❖ Tapestry needle

❖ Fabric for lining or purchased slip

GAUGE

Approx motif measurements as folls:
Motif 1 3"/7.5cm; **motif 2** 3"/7.5cm; **motif 3** 3¼"/8.25cm; **motif 4** 4"/10cm; **motif 5** 5"/12.75cm; **motif 6** 5½"/14cm; **motif 7** 6½"16.5cm
TAKE TIME TO CHECK GAUGE

MOTIF 1

(make 30, plus 2 six-petal motifs)
Ch 6. Join with sl st to form a ring.
Rnd 1 Ch 1, 16 sc in ring. Join with sl st to first sc—16 scs.
Rnd 2 Ch 6 (counts as 1 dc, ch 3), skip next sc, *1 dc in next sc, ch 3, skip next sc; rep from * around. Join with sl st to 3rd ch of beg ch-6—8 ch-3 loops.
Rnd 3 Ch 1, *[1 sc, 1 hdc, 5 dc, l hdc, 1 sc] in next ch-3 sp; rep from * around. Join with sl st to first sc—8 petals.
Fasten off.
Note To make the two 6-petal flower motifs for back shoulder straps, work rnds 1 and 3 same as motif 1 with Rnd 2 as folls: ch 6 (counts as 1 dc, ch 3), skip next 2 sc, *1 dc in next sc, ch 3, skip next 2 sc; rep from * around. Join with sl st to 3rd ch of beg ch-6.

MOTIF 2 (make 16)

Ch 8. Join with sl st to form a ring.
Rnd 1 Ch 1, 12 sc in ring. Join with sl st to first sc—12 sts.
Rnd 2 Ch 1, 1 sc in each sc around. Join with sl st to first sc.
Rnd 3 Ch 6 (counts as 1 tr, ch 2), 1 tr in next sc, ch 2, *1 tr in next sc, ch 2; rep from * around. Join with sl st to 4th ch of beg ch6—12 trs.
Rnd 4 Ch 1, *5 sc in ch-2 sp; rep from * around. Join with sl st to first sc—60 scs.
Fasten off.

My grandmother Annuccia and grandfather Aniello on their wedding day.

MOTIF 3 (make 24)

Ch 8. Join with sl st to form a ring.

Rnd 1 Ch 1, 12 sc in ring. Join with sl st to first sc —12 sts.

Rnd 2 Ch 1, *1 sc in next 2 sc, 2 sc in next sc; rep from * around. Join with sl st in first sc—16 sts.

Rnd 3 Ch 7 (counts as 1 dtr, ch 2), 1 dtr in next sc, *ch 2, 1 dtr in next sc; rep from * around. Join with sl st to 4th ch of beg ch 6—16 trs.

Rnd 4 Ch 1, *5 sc in ch-2 sp; rep from * around. Join with sl st to first sc—80 scs.

Fasten off.

MOTIF 4 (make 25)

Ch 6. Join with sl st to form a ring.

Rnd 1 Ch 4 (counts as 1 tr), 2 tr in ring, [ch 1, 3 tr in ring] 5 times. Join with sl st in top of beg ch-4—18 trs.

Rnd 2 Ch 1, *[2 sc between next 2 tr] twice, 4 sc in ch-1 sp; rep from * around. Join with sl st to first sc—48 scs.

Rnd 3 Ch 1, 1 sc in each sc around. Join with sl st to first sc.

Rnd 4 Ch 4 (counts as 1 tr), 1 tr in next 5 sc, ch 2, *skip next 2 sc, 1 tr in next 6 sc, ch 2; rep from * around. Join with sl st in top of beg ch 4.

Rnd 5 Ch 1, *[2 sc between next 2 tr] 5 times, 4 sc in ch-2 sp; rep from * around. Join with sl st in first sc—84 scs.

Fasten off.

 Medallion Motif Key

 MOTIF 1 (8-PETAL)

 MOTIF 1 (6-PETAL)

 MOTIF 2

 MOTIF 3

 MOTIF 4

MOTIF 5

MOTIF 6

MOTIF 7

MOTIF 5 (make 16)

3-tr (4-tr) cluster *Yo twice, insert hook into next st and draw up a lp, [yo and draw through 2 lps on hook] twice; rep from * 2 (3) times more, yo and draw through all 4 (5) lps on hook.

Ch 12. Join with sl st to form a ring.

Rnd 1 Ch 3 (counts as 1 dc), 21 dc in ring. Join with sl st to first sc—22 dcs.

Rnd 2 Ch 3, 1 dc in each dc around. Join with sl st in top of beg ch-3.

Rnd 3 Ch 4 (counts as 1 tr), 1 tr in same sp, 2 tr in next dc and in each dc around. Join with sl st in top of beg ch-4—44 trs.

Rnd 4 Ch 4, 3-tr cluster over next 3 tr, ch 5, *4-tr cluster over next 4 dc, ch 5; rep from * around. Join with sl st in top of beg ch-4—11 clusters.

Rnd 5 Ch 1, *8 sc in ch-5 lp; rep from * around. Join with sl st to first sc—88 scs.

Fasten off.

❧ *Lovely in lace*

You can wear this dress over a purchased slip or sew your own lining.

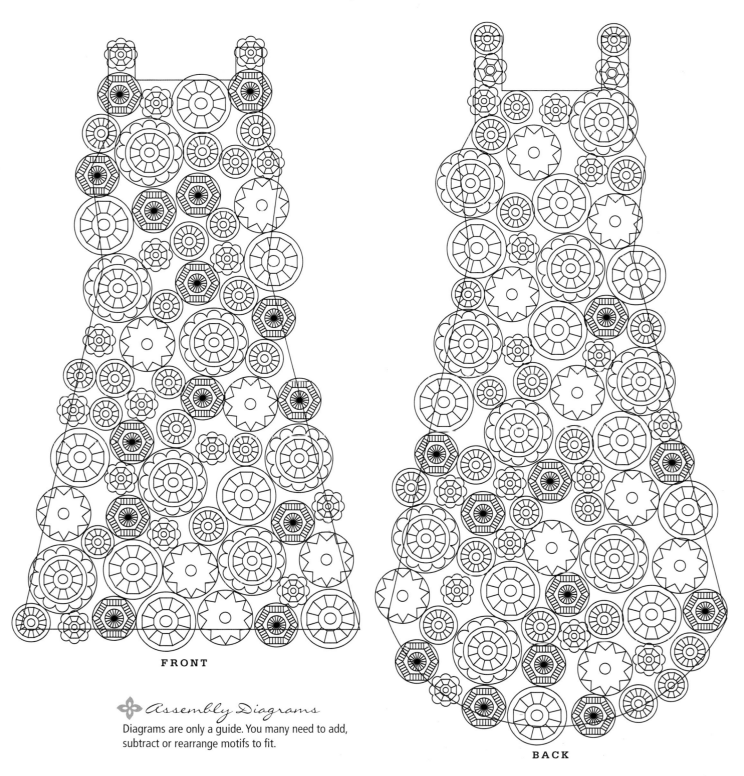

FRONT

BACK

✤ *Assembly Diagrams*
Diagrams are only a guide. You many need to add,
subtract or rearrange motifs to fit.

MOTIF 6 (make 18)

Ch 8. Join with sl st to form a ring.

Rnd 1 Ch 4 (counts as 1 dc, ch 1), [1 dc, ch 1] 11 times in ring. Join with sl st in 3rd ch of beg ch-4 —12 dc.

Rnd 2 Ch 1, 2 sc in each ch-1 sp around. Join with sl st in first sc—24 sts.

Rnd 3 Ch 12 (counts as 1 dtr, ch 7), *skip next sc, 1 dtr in next sc, ch 7; rep from * around. Join with sl st in 5th ch of beg ch-12—12 dtrs.

Rnd 4 Ch 4 (counts as 1 dc, ch 1), [skip next ch, 1 dc in next ch, ch 1] 3 times, *1 dc in next dtr, ch 1, [skip next ch, 1 dc in next ch, ch 1] 3 times; rep from * around. Join with sl st in 3rd ch of beg ch-3—48 dcs.

Rnd 5 Ch 1, 2 sc in each ch-1 sp around. Join with sl st to first sc—96 scs.
Fasten off.

MOTIF 7 (make 16)

Rnds 1–5 Work same as Motif 6.

Rnd 6 *Ch 8, skip next 7 scs, 1 sc in next sc; rep from * around—12 ch-8 lps.

Rnd 7 Ch 1, *[1 sc, 1 hdc, 3 dc, 3 tr, 3dc, 1 hdc, 1 sc] in ch-8 lp; rep from * around. Join with sl st to first sc—12 petals.
Fasten off.

Follow diagrams for motif placement. Sew each piece in place, stretching as necessary to fill gaps. ●

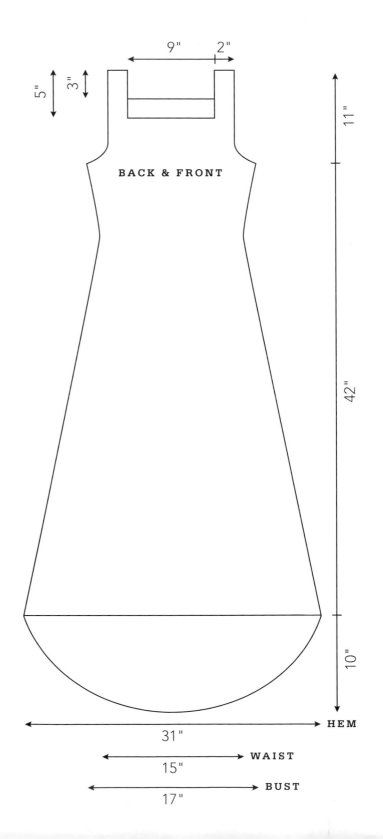

BACK & FRONT

Felted Etruscan Pitcher

Create your own Etruscan artifact with a classic ancient design. Best of all, this self-standing conversation piece can never break.

SIZES
24"/61cm H; 7"/18cm diameter at base/foot; 28"/71cm circumference at widest point in body, after felting

MATERIALS
❖ 2 8oz hanks (each approx 130yd/117m) of Brown Sheep Company *Burley Spun*, 100% wool, in #BS06 deep charcoal (A)

❖ 1 hank #BS181 prairie fire (B)

❖ Size 15 (10mm) 16" and 24" circular needles
OR SIZE TO OBTAIN GAUGE

❖ Size 15 (10mm) double-pointed needles (set of 5)

❖ Tapestry needle

GAUGE
8 sts and 10 rnds = 4"/10cm in St st, before felting
TAKE TIME TO CHECK GAUGE

NOTE
Change to short/long circular needles or dpns as needed.

Starting at top of vase with dpns and A, cast on 42 sts. Distribute over 4 needles as folls:
12 sts on first needle, 10 sts each on 3 needles. Pm and join.

MOUTH
Rnds 1–4 Knit.
Rnd 5 K2tog, k8, ssk (spout), k2, *p2, k2; rep from * to end—40 sts.
Rnd 6 K2tog, k6, ssk, k2, *p2, k2; rep from * to end—38 sts.
Rnd 7 K2tog, k4, ssk, k2, *p2, k2; rep from * to end—36 sts.
Rnd 8 K2tog, k2, ssk, k2, *p2, k2; rep from * to end—34 sts.
Rnd 9 K2tog, ssk, k2, *p2, k2; rep from * to end—32 sts.
Rnd 10 *P2, k2; rep from * to end.
Rep rnd 10 until piece measures 6½"/16.5cm from beg.

BODY
Work rnds 1–29 of Chart. Stitch counts as folls:
40 sts after rnd 11; 48 sts after rnd 14;
56 sts after rnd 21; 64 sts after rnd 24;
72 sts after rnd 27.

Etruscan art has a timeless beauty that has endured over the centuries.

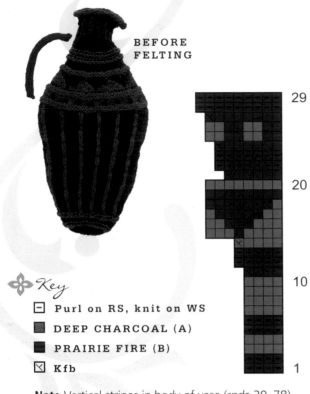

BEFORE FELTING

✤ *Key*

- ⊟ **Purl on RS, knit on WS**
- ▨ **DEEP CHARCOAL (A)**
- ▪ **PRAIRIE FIRE (B)**
- ⊠ **Kfb**

Note Vertical stripes in body of vase (rnds 30–78) are worked in intarsia method. Cut 12 lengths of B, each 3yds/m long.

Rnds 30–48 *K1 B, k5 A; rep from * to end.

Rnd 49 *K1 B, with A, [k1, k2tog, k2]; rep from * to end—60 sts.

Rnds 50–68 *K1 B, k4 A; rep from * to end.

Rnd 69 *K1 B, with A, [k1, k2tog, k1]; rep from * to end—48 sts.

Rnds 70–77 *K1 B, k3 A; rep from * to end.

Rnd 78 *K1 B, with A, [k2tog, k1]; rep from * to end—36 sts.

BASE/FOOT

Rnds 1 and 2 With B, purl.

Rnds 3–6 With A, knit.

Rnds 7 and 8 With B, purl.

Rnd 9 With A, knit.

Rnd 10 *K4, k2tog; rep from * to end—30 sts.

Rnd 11 *K3, k2tog; rep from * to end—24 sts.

Rnd 12 *K2, k2tog; rep from * to end—18 sts.

Rnd 13 *K1, k2tog; rep from * to end—12 sts.

Rnd 14 *K2tog; rep from * to end—6 sts.

Cut yarn, leaving a long tail. Thread tail through rem sts, tighten and secure end.

HANDLE

With A and dpns, cast on 5 sts. Work I-cord (see page 111) for 12½"/32cm. Bind off.

FINISHING

Felt pieces (see page 28). Sew top end of handle between first 2 bands of B and bottom end of handle over rnds 25–26 of Chart. ●

MONTALCINO

Tuscan Sun Shawl

Celebrate the Tuscan sun and shine in this striking shawl that will transport you to a glorious Tuscan hillside.

SIZE

Approx 16"W X 65"L/40.5 x 162.5cm

MATERIALS

❖ 1 50g hank (each approx 100yds/ 90m) of Artyarns *Beaded Silk*, 100% silk with glass gold beads, in #BS134 gold multi (A), 3 hanks in #BS250 white (B) and 3 hanks in #BS231 gold (D)

❖ 6 50g hanks (each approx 163yds/ 146m) of Artyarns *Regal Silk*, 100% silk, in #BS134 gold multi (C)

❖ Size 5 (3.75mm) needles, OR SIZE TO OBTAIN GAUGE

❖ Tapestry needle

GAUGE

A, B and D motifs measure approx 8"/20.5cm in diameter
C motifs measure approx 7"/18cm in diameter
TAKE TIME TO CHECK GAUGE

SUN MOTIF

Make 21 motifs: 1 with A, 5 with B, 10 with C and 5 with D.
Cast on 22 sts.
Row 1 K7, turn.
Row 2 K7, turn.
Row 3 Bind off 1 st, k next 8 sts, turn.
Row 4 K9, turn.
Row 5 Bind off 1 st, k next 10 sts, turn.
Row 6 K11, turn.
Row 7 Bind off 1 st, k next 12 sts, turn.
Row 8 K13, turn.
Row 9 Bind off 1 st, k next 14 sts, turn.
Row 10 K15, turn.
Row 11 Bind off 1 st, k next 16 sts, turn.
Row 12 K17, cast on 5 sts—22 sts.
Rep rows 1–12 seventeen times more, then rows 1–11 once.

Bind off all sts, leaving a long tail. Sew cast-on edge to bound-off edge, then pick up each ridge in center of motif, draw tight and secure. Place motifs as desired in a roughly rectangular shape, overlapping as desired, and sew each motif in place. ●

Motif Key

GOLD MULTI WITH BEADS (A)
make 1

WHITE (B)
make 5

GOLD MULTI (C)
make 10

GOLD (D)
make 5

Assembly Diagram

Tuscan Food and Wine

Of all the wonderful regional cuisines in Italy, Tuscan is one of my favorites. The secret to the success of Tuscan dishes is their simplicity. The ingredients are fresh, resulting in strong, honest, delicious flavors that do not require heavy sauces or excessive seasoning. Light use of salt, pepper, basil, rosemary, tarragon, sage and oregano brings dishes to life when you add the magic elixir: Tuscan olive oil.

Tuscan olive oil is perhaps the finest in the world, and just dipping a piece of wonderful Tuscan bread in the oil can be a culinary delight. (Tuscan bread is made without salt and can seem bland at first, but get it together with the olive oil, and *mama mia!*) In autumn, another distinctive flavor to savor is the elusive and expensive *tartufo* (truffle), which is worth every euro.

A traditional Tuscan meal is a leisurely affair (lasting two to three hours) with an *antipasto* (appetizer), *primo piatto* (first course of pasta or soup), *secondo piatto* (second course of meat or fish) and *contorno* (side dish), all accompanied by a fabulous Tuscan wine and followed by a *dolce* (dessert), *caffè* and grappa (a strong digestive after-dinner drink). But don't feel compelled to indulge in this *abbondanza*; you can order just one or two courses without incurring the raised eyebrow of your waiter (Italians are very *simpatico*).

ANTIPASTI

Affettati misti are delicious mixed cured meats, including salami, *capacolla* and prosciutto. *Crostini misti* are small pieces of toast topped with pâtés or pastes, such as liver, anchovy, olive and tomato. *Bruschetta* is toasted bread rubbed with garlic, olive oil and salt and often covered with diced tomatoes.

PRIMI PIATTI

Ribollita is a thick soup made with cabbage, beans, herbs, tomatoes, various vegetables and chunks of bread. It's a meal in itself and is absolutely delicious—every version will taste different. *Pici* (or *pinci*) is a thick, handmade pasta indigenous to Tuscany and served with tomato-, *cinghiale*- (wild boar) or truffle-based sauce.

Don't miss it! *Pappardelle* are broad noodles usually served with *lepre* (hare) or *cinghiale* sauce. *Strozzapreti* (literally "priest stranglers") are pasta dumplings served with various sauces. Legend has it that priests loved them so much they would choke on them as they gorged themselves, so be sure to exercise restraint!

SECONDI PIATTI

Tuscans are meat-eaters. The meat is usually grilled over open fire and seasoned with herbs and olive oil. *Bistecca alla fiorentina* is the king of steaks. It's cut very thick and Tuscans like it rare, but don't be afraid to order it more well done. *Arista di maiale* is a sliced roast pork loin. *Delizioso! Scottiglia di cinghiale* is a beautiful, rich stew made with wild boar. It's one of my favorites, and I have a hard time not ordering it whenever I see it on the menu. *Arrosto misto* is a country dish of mixed roasted meats that can include beef, pork, chicken, lamb, duck and sausage, with vegetables. *Baccalà* is a tasty dried salt cod usually cooked with garlic, parsley and tomatoes.

CONTORNI

One of my favorite side dishes is *fiori di zucca fritti* (fried zucchini blossoms)—a little bit of heaven! My Italian grandmother made these for me when I was a little girl, and if you can find them on a menu, you must order them. They are lightly breaded, deep-fried and sprinkled with Parmesan cheese. Beans are an absolute staple in Tuscany and are used in many, many dishes. *Fagioli al fiasco* is a dish made with beans cooked al dente in a flask over hot embers and served with just olive oil and black pepper. It is pure Tuscany, and when you finish a bowl, you'll be able to speak fluent Italian.

❧ *Mangia, mangia, mangia!*

Tuscan food is sublimely simple, yet seriously scrumptious.
In Tuscany, dining is an art that everyone savors.

DOLCI

Cantucci are twice-baked almond cookies that are dipped in a sweet dessert wine called *vin santo* (holy wine). Each town has its own version of the cookie. *Panforte* is a dark and dense fruitcake spiced with cloves and cinnamon. *Panforte* from Siena is especially delicious. Chestnuts are very popular in Tuscany and show up in all kinds of desserts. *Castagne ubriache* are chestnuts covered in red wine sauce (hence the name, which means "drunken chestnuts") and baked custard. Don't forget Tuscan cheeses like pecorino (sheep's milk) in a honey and pepper sauce (to die for) or ricotta (sheep's or cow's milk whey cheese) with a touch of honey. And then there's *gelato,* Italy's famous soft, dense ice cream sold in *gelaterie* throughout Tuscany in a veritable rainbow of delectable flavors.

WINES

Italy has some of the finest wines in the world, and Tuscany has some of the best wines in Italy. The warm Mediterranean climate and sunny hillsides of Tuscany are perfect for the growing of grapes. The most famous of Tuscan wines, Chianti, is no longer the modest little wine in a straw-covered bottle. Many Chianti Classico wines rank with the finest in the world. They are delicious and food-friendly. Brunello di Montalcino wines are produced from a variety of Sangiovese grape grown around the town of Montalcino. They have a deep color and are full-bodied and balanced. These reds are my favorites. Vino Nobile di Montepulciano is an intense wine with plummy fruit and smooth tannins. Super Tuscans are a relatively new variety of wines. They are powerful wines that command powerful prices. Sangiovese and Cabernet Sauvignon combine to produce a Super Tuscan called Tignanello. Vernaccia di San Gimignano is a white wine from the town of San Gimignano that is delightfully dry with notes of honey. It's great on a warm day. Grappa is a high-powered, clear after-dinner brandy made from the skins and residue of grapes. The best grappa can be a great after-dinner digestive, and a lesser one can take the enamel off your teeth. If grappa is too strong, try *limoncello,* a very nice lemon-based, chilled liqueur. But remember, you don't have to order any of these varieties to enjoy Tuscan wine. Simply order a glass or pitcher of the *vino della casa* (house wine), and if you're sitting on a terrace overlooking a beautiful Tuscan landscape, it will taste like the best wine in the world.●

EXPLORING

A Visit to Antica Macelleria Cecchini

After taking in the works of Tuscany's greatest painters, sculptors and architects, it's time to enjoy the talents of another artist: Dario Cecchini, whose butcher shop, Antica Macelleria Cecchini, in the tiny town of Panzano in Chianti (Via XX Luglio 11), is a major tourist attraction. Dario has been called "the Michelangelo of beef," and his dedication to serving the best meats in Tuscany has earned him a reputation and celebrity status worthy of a movie star. His quality products are served in some of the finest restaurants in Italy.

But it is not only his professional skills that have endeared Dario to people around the world; it is his enormous charisma. He openly shares his optimistic philosophy on life with his customers and quotes passages from Dante as he skillfully carves up a *porchetta.*

Dario's family has owned the butcher shop for 250 years. Music is always playing, and there is a festive air throughout the store. On the day we visited, it was filled with locals and tourists enjoying samples of sausages, cold cuts, *polpettone di manzo* (an amazing Tuscan meatloaf), cheese, bread and wine. The aroma in the shop was intoxicating. We left with a sack full of

cold cuts, cheese and bread that we enjoyed that evening with a bottle of lovely local Chianti, seated on the terrace of our hotel overlooking a breathtaking Tuscan landscape. Life is tough! ●

Knitter-Friendly Recipes

Try one of these easy and *delizioso* recipes, open a bottle of Brunello, pop in a CD of Andrea Bocelli, and you're dining in Tuscany! (Well, almost.)

EGGPLANT CAPONATA
Makes approximately 6 cups; serves 12 as an appetizer

❖ Sometimes referred to as "poor man's caviar," this table relish is a delicious spread for bread or crackers. There are about 70,000 variations, but I love this one for its sheer simplicity.

1 large eggplant, unpeeled and cut into 1-inch dice
2½ cups onions, chopped
1 6-oz can tomato paste
¼ cup water
2 Tbsp sugar
1 tsp salt
1 tsp black pepper
½ cup pimiento-stuffed olives
½ cup extra-virgin olive oil
1 cup celery, diced
½ cup red-wine vinegar
1 large garlic clove, chopped

1 Combine all ingredients in large mixing bowl. Stir well and pour into 2-quart glass casserole dish; cover with lid.
2 Microwave on full power for 10 minutes. After 10 minutes, uncover (be careful of steam) and stir.
3 Cover and microwave for 10–15 minutes more, until all vegetables are tender.
4 Cool completely and serve as an appetizer with crackers, chips or Italian bread. (Caponata can also be refrigerated and served chilled.)

PASTA FRITTATA
Serves 12

❖ This is the perfect way to use up any leftover pasta and sauce you have in the fridge. It tastes fabulous and takes less than 20 minutes from start to finish! Make this for dinner in a hurry—when you must get back to that knitting project! (Recipe can be cut in half.)

8 eggs
8 cups cold pasta with any leftover sauce
1½ cups grated pecorino romano cheese
Salt and freshly ground pepper to taste
½ cup extra-virgin olive oil, divided

1 In large mixing bowl beat eggs. Season generously with salt and pepper.
2 Fold beaten eggs into pasta and sauce; add cheese and mix until very well blended. Hint: Mixing with your hands works well.
3 In a large, nonstick skillet over medium-high, heat ¼ cup oil. Pour pasta mixture into pan and cook for about 5–7 minutes. DO NOT STIR.
4 Place a large plate over the skillet and, holding skillet handle and plate firmly with oven mitts, invert the skillet contents onto the plate.
5 Return skillet to stovetop, add remaining oil and heat to moderately hot. Carefully slide frittata back into skillet and cook 5–7 minutes more, until crisp and brown.
6 Remove to serving dish, cut into wedges and serve either hot or cold.

MARIE'S SECRET PIGNOLI COOKIES
Makes approximately 2 dozen cookies

❖ A simple variation on these cookies is called Angelic Cookies. Just leave out the confectioners' sugar and pine nuts and follow all other instructions.

1 cup granulated sugar
1 7-oz package almond paste
1 tsp amaretto (almond-flavored liqueur—the secret ingredient) or 1 tsp vanilla extract
2 large egg whites
¼ cup confectioners' sugar
¼ cup pine nuts
Parchment paper (or greased aluminum foil) for lining cookie sheet

1 Preheat oven to 350 degrees F.
2 Place sugar and almond paste in a large bowl. Beat with mixer at medium speed until almond paste is broken into pieces.
3 Add confectioners' sugar, amaretto and egg whites and beat at high speed for 4 minutes or until smooth. Chill batter for 20 minutes.
4 Drop batter by teaspoons 1 inch apart on parchment-lined baking sheet (or greased aluminum foil). Sprinkle pine nuts on top.
5 Bake for 10 minutes until edges of cookies are light golden brown. (Do not overcook or cookies will get hard.) Cool completely on baking sheets. Carefully remove from sheets and cool on racks.

Nicky's Travel Tips

This book is based on my personal experiences, and I hope my insights will be helpful to you, but I strongly recommend that you invest in one or more travel guides to Tuscany. They will greatly enhance your trip and give you lots more options. The Frommer's, Fodor's and Eyewitness guides to Tuscany all provide invaluable, in-depth information. Here are just a few more tips to help make your trip as smooth and enjoyable as possible. *Buon viaggio!*

PASSPORTS

Apply for a passport well in advance of your trip, because you won't get far without one. And don't be discouraged by the photo, even though most of them make you look like your yarn shop just informed you they no longer carry the yarn you need to complete your sweater.

PLANNING YOUR TRIP

The best times to travel to Tuscany are spring and fall. If you go in the summer, you'll encounter heat, long lines and lots of other tourists, especially in the cities. Spend some time choosing locations to visit, and try to keep the trip leisurely—this is a vacation, after all. If you rent a car, plot your trip on Mapquest.com, which is amazingly accurate in Tuscany.

PACKING

Before you leave, put all your clothes and all your money on the bed. Take half the clothes and twice the money!

GETTING TO TUSCANY

There are two international airports in Tuscany: in Pisa and Florence. The airport in Pisa is larger, but I like to fly into Florence, because it is more central. There are no direct flights to Florence from the United States.

DRIVING, ITALIAN-STYLE

There are many trains and buses in Tuscany, but the best way to discover the country is to rent a car. Once you get over the organized chaos of Italian driving, you'll be glad you did. Take a cab from the airport into Florence (you don't need or want a car there), and after your stay there, return to the airport to rent a car and hit the road. Shop online for bargains. Italians drive aggressively, so just take your time, drive defensively and be prepared to accept the international single-digit salute as they pass you.

MONEY

The currency in Italy is the euro. ATMs are everywhere (even in small towns) and are the best local source of currency, but credit cards and traveler's checks are accepted. Bring enough euros from the U.S. for transportation from the airport and miscellaneous minor costs.

LANGUAGE

Learning a few Italian phrases will go a long way toward making your trip easier, and the locals will appreciate the effort. A few helpful words and phrases include *buon giorno* (good morning), *grazie* (thank you), *per favore* (please), *Dov'è il bagno per donne?* (Where is the ladies' room?) and *Quanto costa questo filato?* (How much is this yarn?).

KNITTING

If you want to bring your knitting with you, pack your needles in your checked baggage. I once lost a good pair to airport security in Florence when I tried to carry them on. Or visit one of the yarn shops I describe in the Florence and Siena sections of this book and start a project when you're over there to enjoy the full knitting-in-Tuscany experience.

And finally, you're not in Kansas anymore. Appreciate the differences you find instead of resenting them. You're a guest in their country and you represent America and the International Order of Knitters. Go to Tuscany with an open mind, and you're sure to be enchanted. And remember, it's time to go home when you start looking like your passport photo! ●

Yarn and Notions Resources

Alchemy Yarns of Transformation
P.O. Box 1080
Sebastopol, CA 95473
www.alchemyyarns.com

Artyarns
39 Westmoreland Avenue
White Plains, NY 10606
www.artyarns.com

Berroco, Inc.
P.O. Box 367
14 Elmdale Road
Uxbridge, MA 01569
www.berroco.com

Brown Sheep Company
100662 County Road 16
Mitchell, NE 69357
www.brownsheep.com

Cascade Yarns
1224 Andover Park East
Tukwila, WA 98188
www.cascadeyarns.com

Chianti Cashmere
www.chianticashmere.com

Colinette
Distributed by Unique
Kolours, Ltd.
www.colinette.com

Dale of Norway
4750 Shelburne Road
Shelburne VT 05482
www.dale.no

Fairmount Fibers, Ltd.
915 North 28th Street
Philadelphia, PA 19130
www.fairmountfibers.com

Fiesta Yarns
5401 San Diego NE
Albuquerque, NM 87113
www.fiestayarns.com

GGH
Distributed by Muench Yarns
www.ggh-garn.com

Jade Sapphire Exotic Fibres
866-857-3897
www.jadesapphire.com

Lacis
2982 Adeline Street
Berkeley, CA 94703
www.lacis.com

Louet North America
USA: 808 Commerce Park
Station VO
Ogdensburg, NY 13669
Canada: 3425 Hands Road
Prescott, Ontario
Canada K0E 1T0
www.louet.com

Manos del Uruguay
Distributed by Fairmount
Fibers, Ltd.
www.manosdeluruguay
.co.uk

Muench Yarns
1323 Scott Street
Petaluma, CA 94954
www.muenchyarns.com

The Old Mill Knitting Company
P.O. Box 81176
961 Gerner Road East
Ancaster, Ontario
Canada L9G 3K9
www.oldmillknitting.com

Rowan
Distributed by Westminster
Fibers, Inc.
UK: Green Lane Mill
Holmfirth
England HD9 2DX
www.knitrowan.com

Sunbelt Fastener Co.
8841 Exposition Boulevard
Culver City, CA 90230
www.sunbeltfastener.com

Tilli Tomas
617-524-3330
www.tillitomas.com

Trendsetter Yarns
USA: 16745 Saticoy Street
Suite #101
Van Nuys, CA 91406
Canada: Distributed by The
Old Mill Knitting Company
www.trendsetteryarns.com

Unique Kolours, Ltd.
28 North Bacton Hill Road
Malvern, PA 19355
www.uniquekolours.com

Westminster Fibers, Inc.
165 Ledge Street
Nashua, NH 03060
www.westminsterfibers.com

Compasses on page 6
Top left:
Desk Compass
Item #18M03.01
Lower right:
Small Marching Compass
Item #18M02.01
Both available at
www.garrettwade.com
800-221-2942

Abbreviations

approx	approximately	**pg(s)**	page(s)
beg	begin(s)(ning)	**pm**	place marker
ch	chain	**psso**	pass slipped stitch over
cm	centimeter	**rem**	remain
cont	continue(d)(s)	**rep**	repeat
dc(s)	double crochet(s)	**rev**	reverse
dec(s)	decrease(s)	**rnd(s)**	round(s)
dpn(s)	double-pointed needle(s)	**RS**	right side
dtr	double triple crochet	**sc(s)**	single crochet
est	establish(ed)	**sk2p**	slip 1 knitwise, k2tog, pass slipped st over
foll	follow(ing)(s)	**s2kp**	slip 2 knitwise one at a time, k1, pass 2 slipped sts over the k1
g	grams		
hdc	half double crochet		
inc(s)	increase(s)	**sl st**	slip stitch
k	knit	**sp**	space
kfb	knit in front and back of stitch	**ssk**	slip 2 knitwise one at a time, insert left-hand needle into slipped sts and k2tog tbl
L	length		
lp(s)	loop(s)		
m	meters		
MB	make bobble	**St st**	stockinette stitch
m1	make one st by lifting bar between sts, twist and k tbl	**st(s)**	stitch(es)
		tbl	through back loop
mm	milimeters	**tog**	together
mult	multiple	**tr(s)**	triple crochet(s)
patt(s)	pattern(s)	**W**	width
pfb	purl in front and back of stitch	**WS**	wrong side
		yd(s)	yard(s)
		yo	yarn over

Skill Levels

BEGINNER
Perfect for new knitters, these items use basic stitches and minimal shaping.

EASY
These projects feature basic stitches, repetitive stitch patterns, simple color changes and simple shaping and finishing.

INTERMEDIATE
These projects use a variety of techniques or mid-level shaping.

EXPERIENCED
For more experienced knitters, these projects feature intricate stitch patterns, more advanced techniques or detailed shaping.

Knitting and Embroidery Techniques

THREE-NEEDLE BIND-OFF

This bind-off is used to join two edges that have the same number of stitches, such as shoulder edges, and which have been placed on holders.

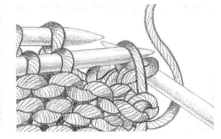

1 With the right side of the two pieces facing each other, and the needles parallel, insert a third needle knitwise into the first stitch of each needle. Wrap the yarn around the needle as if to knit.

2 Knit these two stitches together and slip them off the needles. *Knit the next two stitches together in the same way as shown.

3 Slip the first stitch on the third needle over the second stitch and off the needle. Repeat from the * in step 2 across the row until all the stitches are bound off.

DUPLICATE STITCH

Duplicate stitch covers a knit stitch. Bring the needle up below the stitch to be worked. Insert the needle under both loops one row above and pull it through. Insert it back into the stitch below and through the center of the next stitch in one motion, as shown.

I-CORD OR KNIT CORD

Using 2 double-pointed needles, cast on 3 to 5 stitches. *Knit one row on RS. Without turning the work, slip the stitches to right end of needle to work the next row on the RS. Repeat from * until desired length. Bind off.

FRENCH KNOT

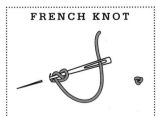

STEM STITCH

Ciao, Bella!

Mille grazie to: Trisha Malcolm and the amazing staff at Sixth&Spring Books whose hard work and combination of editorial expertise, aesthetic appreciation and terrific talent helped create this *bellissimo* book: Wendy Williams (the lovely guiding light at the end of the tunnel), Diane Lamphron (putting the "art" in art direction), Michelle Bredeson (documenting the details), Joe Vior (a never-ending fountain of creativity), Julie Hines (a stylish stylist), Tanis Gray (my favorite yarn editor) and Kristina Sigler (copy editor extraordinaire).

Rose Callahan for the lovely fashion photography and Howard Epstein for additional photos.

The gang at Southpaw—Dave Viccaro, Jeff Pattie, Farah Pidgeon and Nick Michael—for many of the vintage fashions.

My talented, non-Italian knitters: Jo Brandon, Eileen Curry, Nancy Henderson and Eva Wilkens.

My big Italian-American family and all my friends who made this project very personal.

The beautiful, warm people I met in Tuscany who were so generous.

My ever-supportive fans, students and readers who I hope will enjoy this journey.

My editorial advisor, travel companion, wine expert and husband, Howard, at lunch in Greve in Chianti.